GEMSTONES & MINERALS
OF AUSTRALIA

Golden rutile crystals in quartz (magnified); Tingha, NSW.

GEMSTONES & MINERALS
OF AUSTRALIA

Lin & Gayle Sutherland

This edition published in 2014.

Published in 2000 by Reed New Holland Publishers
Sydney • Auckland

Level 1, 178 Fox Valley Road, Wahroonga, NSW 2076, Australia
5/39 Woodside Ave Northcote, Auckland 0627 New Zealand

newhollandpublishers.com

A record of this book is held at the British Library and the National Library of Australia.

ISBN 9781921517297

Group Managing Director: Fiona Schultz
Project Editor: Jodi De Vantier
Designer: Tracy Loughlin
Cover design: Lorena Susak
Cover Image: Galaxy Opal, by Jim Frasier
Production Director: Arlene Gippert
Printed in China

Keep up with Reed New Holland
and New Holland Publishers

 ReedNewHolland
 @NewHollandPublishers and @ReedNewHolland

ACKNOWLEDGMENTS

This guide draws on the photographic strengths of two major contributors. Dr Jim Frazier supplied most of the gemstone and some mineral photography. The other source was the photographic staff of the Australian Museum. Over the last 50 years they have photographed a large range of minerals and gemstones in the museum collection and these provide most of the selected mineral illustrations. Rudy Weber, from Gem Studies Laboratory, Sydney, kindly provided additional gemstone photographs. Other photographs came from Dr Mary E. White, Sydney, the two authors and some isolated sources.

Most of the specimens used to illustrate the guide comes from the Australian Museum collections, including the Albert Chapman mineral collection. The Australian Museum Trust and Executive are thanked for permission to use collection material in this project. Dr Peter Williams, University of Western Sydney, and Dr Peter Bayliss, Australian Museum, advised on updated mineral names and literature sources for this revised edition.

Faceted sapphires, Anakie, Qld.

CONTENTS

INTRODUCTION

This is a guide to Australia's treasure chest—its gems and minerals. Gemstones are minerals, which are the natural chemicals that make up rocks. However, not all minerals are gemstones. Gem minerals are rare, superior examples of the mineral world. Hence they are desired for their beauty or special effects. Some other gem materials, such as amber and pearls have a biological origin. In the widest sense, gem materials range far beyond natural materials, many now being synthesised in laboratories. Most synthetic gemstones are replicas of their mineral equivalents, but others, such as cubic zirconia, are not found in nature. Gemstones also inspire imitations in a variety of materials. Because gemstones are prized for their beauty and rarity, they are valuable and their use is one of the world's oldest industries. One superb, natural gemstone may be valued at millions of dollars, while another that looks similar or is an artificial equivalent, may be bought as a cheap trinket. So, in dealing with gemstones we are stepping into a complex world of human endeavour.

In the mineral world, gemstones represent only a fraction of Earth's offerings. In general, minerals form a great natural resource that has supported humans through many civilisations. They are a driving force in international economic activities. Some people collect gemstones and minerals for their aesthetic appeal or as examples of the natural world. This guide is aimed at helping such people recognise a range of gems and minerals, concentrating on Australian examples. The Australian continent is rich in gem and mineral resources and for some it is world-renowned.

Gem concentrate, Barrington Tops, NSW.

ABOUT THIS BOOK

Not every mineral found in Australia is included in this guide, but it does cover a large number of the more common minerals, some rarities and the odd curiosity. Some minerals are either similar to those already depicted here or are found in minor amounts in rocks. An example of the latter is monazite, a phosphate mineral, rich in rare earth elements, that is associated with granitic rocks. Other relatively widespread silicate minerals are not included because of space limitations. These include the feldspathoid minerals, which resemble the feldspars but have less silicon in their silicate framework. Nepheline, a sodium aluminium silicate, and leucite, a potassium aluminium silicate, are the two main representatives. Other minerals missing from the guide have restricted distribution in Australia or have little current economic exploitation. Examples include mineral alloys of iridium and osmium, which sparked a mining rush in Tasmania in the early 1900s. Others are relatively well-known simple chemicals, such as halite (salt), graphite, sulfur and mercury. Readers wishing

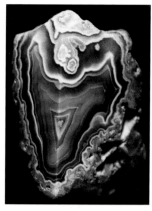

'Map of Tasmania' agate from the Lune River, Tas.

to explore the full diversity of Australian minerals and gemstones can consult material available from Federal and State mineral-based institutions, libraries, journals and online sources (see p. 130).

Australian gemstones are showcased first in the guide, as an enticing way to enter the vital but sometimes less glamorous mineral offerings of the continent. The gemstones are arranged according to the gem mineral species and their varieties. The minerals are organised differently, according to the main metallic element or elements in their chemical composition. This is an arrangement of convenience rather than a strictly systematic approach and some minerals could be placed equally under one or more elements. However, it does provide a grouping that reveals the economic importance of many minerals. In most mineral descriptions, the elements in its composition are listed rather than the detailed formula. Exact mineral formulae can be found in mineral textbooks, glossaries and online sources.

Each main gemstone and mineral category includes a map of its distribution in Australia, to provide an overall image of the mineral wealth held in this continent. Many areas, although not providing valuable gem deposits, nevertheless furnish a good selection of lapidary materials, such as agate and petrified wood. These have much popular appeal and people like to read all sorts of significance into the patterns they find, such as seeing the shape of Tasmania in a Tasmanian agate! The majority of specimens photographed in the guide come from the Australian Museum collection, where a considerable number of them are displayed in the public galleries. The dimensions or weight (in carats) of specimens are given in the Specimen Details on pages 130–38.

Introduction

This guide focuses primarily on mineral specimens that are likely to be of interest to the non-specialist. For this reason, more specialised areas of interest—such as studying micromounts, which are tiny specimens studied under microscopes—are not included here. The authors have attempted to balance popular terminology with the latest mineral nomenclature as approved by the International Mineralogical Association. Although not a buyer's guide to gems, this book also provides some useful tips for buying gemstones on page 129.

At 12.76 carats, the Argyle Pink Jubilee diamond made history as Australia's largest pink diamond crystal.

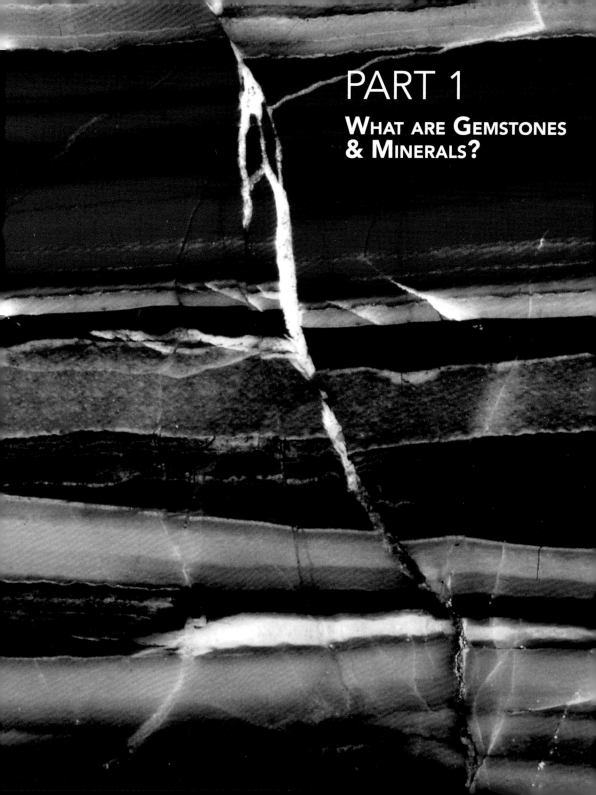

PART 1

WHAT ARE GEMSTONES & MINERALS?

MINERAL BASICS

Chemical and Crystal Duet The two basic aspects of a mineral are its chemical composition and its crystal character. This helps in recognising the many different minerals found in rocks. Although over 6,600 known minerals exist in nature, most are rare and only a few hundred minerals are relatively common. Like many other natural entities, minerals have their own laws, which have a logic and beauty in their intrinsic organisation.

On the chemical side, the most common mineral is quartz, which is made up of the elements silicon (Si) and oxygen (O). These being relatively light elements, one can expect quartz to be a relatively light mineral. To balance the electrical charges on the atoms of these two different elements, two oxygen atoms combine with every silicon atom, which gives a chemical budget or formula of SiO_2 (silica). This is a relatively simple formula, but other minerals may contain many different elements, leading to complex mineral compositions.

On the crystal side, quartz holds these two elements in a rigid arrangement throughout the mineral. This specific arrangement becomes reflected in the external shape of the mineral, called a crystal. The crystal shape is made up of a series of flat faces, but it is important to realise that these natural faces are distinct from the faces or facets that are cut into a gemstone to enhance its attractive properties. With quartz, no matter how much the crystal shape is complicated by extra faces, it will always show a set of faces that appears three times when the crystal is rotated around its main axis. This triple symmetry is characteristic of the trigonal crystal system. Altogether there are seven crystal systems, in which each mineral finds a place.

Each mineral species has this duality of chemical and crystal nature. Quartz, for example, has the same chemistry as two rarer minerals, cristobalite and tridymite, but each has a different crystal structure because they form under different temperature and pressure conditions. Cristobalite shows one set of crystal faces that is seen four times in a turn of the crystal, a characteristic of the tetragonal crystal system. Tridymite shows three sets of faces that appear twice, when the crystal is turned on each three-dimensional axis, a characteristic of the orthorhombic crystal system.

Chemical and Crystal Complications

Needless to say many other factors can complicate the final chemistry and crystal shape of a mineral, so its recognition needs to take account of many potential variations in appearance. Firstly, stray amounts of other elements may enter into its basic chemical make up. This allows the mineral a greater chemical range and some flexibility in its nature, which may influence its colours. Secondly, particular growth conditions can produce wide variations in appearance.

Another complication is twinning. In these cases the mineral has an equal opportunity to grow in separate crystal directions and so produces a mirror-shaped twinned crystal. The twinning process can be simple, as in gypsum, which forms an arrow-like shape with a notched tail. Such notches are typical of twinned crystals. Other twinning can be very complex and repetitive, as in chabazite. This mineral basically forms asymmetric, rhomb-shaped crystals. However twinning can modify the shape by forming crystals that are rounded or flattened in shape. In some twinned crystals, the twins appear to pass through each other in different directions and these are known as interpenetrant twins. However, experienced mineral identifiers become familiar with these tricks of nature and find that, despite such complications, the basic nature of the mineral still remains.

The final factor in recognising a mineral is understanding the limitations placed on its growth by nature. Under suitable conditions, with adequate space for growth, many minerals will form fine crystals with fully developed crystal faces. Where crystals form in crowded conditions, or too quickly to develop their final shapes, they show an irregular crystalline or partly cystallised condition. Vein quartz is a good example. In other cases, crystals grow too small to be visible and form in a microcrystalline mass. In quartz, this gives rise to the chalcedony varieties. Finally, some minerals are incapable of forming a proper crystal structure and are amorphous or devoid of structure. Opaline silica is a good example and its lack of structure allows some water to be held within the mineral. Nature produces many examples of mineral perfection, but far more often crystals become distorted or intergrown, so that the textbook examples do not always apply.

WHAT ARE GEMSTONES?

As few as 20 minerals are commonly cut and polished into gemstones and fewer than 200 are ever cut, even as curiosities for collectors. This is a very small proportion of the many thousand minerals so far identified. To be cut as a gem and worn, a mineral must be hard enough to survive abrasion, which at once eliminates a great number. It must be beautiful for some feature—usually colour, clarity, surface patterning or internal inclusions. The rich, red colour of ruby, the colourless brilliance of diamond, the colour play of precious opal and the golden spangles in sunstone are all considered beautiful in their own distinctive way. As well as being beautiful and durable, a potential gem mineral must occur in sizes large enough to cut and in deposits generous enough to warrant mining. These restrictions greatly narrow the field and bring us to another aspect of gems that makes them precious—rarity.

Besides minerals, plants and animals have supplied us with gem materials over the ages. Amber, a fossil resin from ancient trees; pearls formed by oysters and other molluscs; coral which forms a branching support for marine polyp colonies; shells; jet, which is a type of coal; and even fossils themselves, such as ammonites, have all been worn as adornments since the beginning of human history. Natural glasses, such as tektites, which are meteoritic impact glasses, and obsidians, which are volcanic glasses, have long been used in jewellery.

THE CRYSTAL SYSTEMS

CUBIC A crystal system (also called isometric) with the highest order of symmetry of the seven systems: three axes of equal length, intersecting each other at right angles. There are thirteen axes of symmetry, nine planes of symmetry and a centre of symmetry.

prism and pyramid

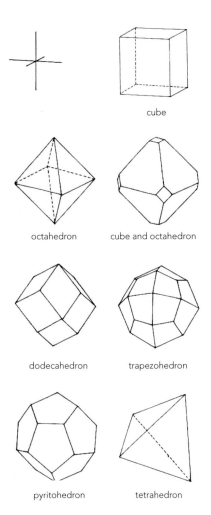

cube

octahedron

cube and octahedron

dodecahedron

trapezohedron

pyritohedron

tetrahedron

TETRAGONAL A crystal system with three axes. Two are of equal length, at right angles to each other. The third axis is longer or shorter than the other two and is at right angles to them. There are five axes of symmetry, five planes of symmetry and a centre of symmetry.

hexagonal prism

HEXAGONAL A crystal system with four axes: three lateral ones intersecting at 60 degrees on the same plane and a principal axis at 90 degrees to the others. There are seven axes of symmetry, seven planes of symmetry and a centre of symmetry.

rhombohedron

TRIGONAL A crystal system with four axes arranged as in the hexagonal system but with lower symmetry. The usual symmetry is one axis of symmetry, three planes of symmetry and a centre of symmetry..

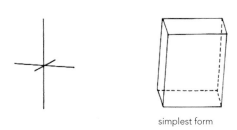

simplest form

ORTHORHOMBIC A crystal system with three axes, all of different lengths, at right angles to each other. There are three axes of symmetry, three planes of symmetry and a centre of symmetry.

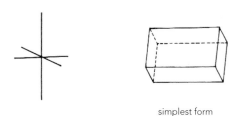

simplest form

MONOCLINIC A crystal system with three axes of different lengths. Two are inclined to each other at an angle other than 90°. The third axis is at right angles to the other two. There is one axis of symmetry, a plane of symmetry and a centre of symmetry.

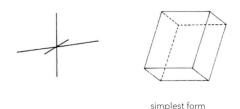

simplest form

TRICLINIC A crystal system with three axes, none of equal length and none at 90° to another. There is a centre of symmetry but no axes or planes of symmetry.

Past and Present In earlier centuries, gemstones were in very short supply and were used to adorn the powerful or the exalted. Today, because of sophisticated exploration and mining technology and the increased affluence of whole populations, ordinary people can afford to buy gemstones and many own at least one diamond.

Over the centuries, many new minerals and gemstones have been discovered and this process still continues, with new varieties and new colours being uncovered by widespread exploration. More recently, important new gemstones have been discovered. In 1906, the first blue crystals of an unknown mineral were found in San Benito County, California, and subsequently given the name benitoite. This rare and attractive gemstone occurs mainly at that locality and has since become sought-after by collectors. In 1945, a new and extremely rare gemstone was discovered, not in the ground, but as a cut stone in a jeweller's box of odds and ends. After investigation, this mystery stone was found to be a new mineral and was named taaffeite after its discoverer, Count Taaffe, a Dublin gemmologist. In 1967, a new, violet-blue gem variety of the mineral zoisite was discovered and later named tanzanite, after its locality in Tanzania. Then, in 1974, a beautiful, new, bright green garnet was introduced to the world as tsavorite, named after the Tsavo National Park, in Kenya, where it was found. Unusual colours in known gemstones and new gem qualities of hitherto non-gem minerals are continually uncovered.

Some gems of biological origin have become rare because their supply has dwindled. The trade in elephant ivory was internationally banned in 1989, due to worldwide concern for declining elephant populations. Legitimate ivory goods are still produced in countries with an abundant supply of fossil mammoth ivory, such as Canada and Russia. Coral, particularly red coral from the Mediterranean, is similarly threatened by depletion, with the best red quality now rare. Natural pearls are not in sufficient supply for the growing world market and most pearls are now cultured.

Australia supplies most of the world's opals and pink diamonds, as well as many of the world's blue sapphires. Many other fine gem varieties are found here and Australian South Sea cultured pearls are of the highest quality and sought-after internationally.

IDENTIFYING MINERALS

There is more to a mineral than meets the eye. Superficially a mineral can exhibit many guises, so its physical properties become the main guide to recognition. Colour can be a help and a hindrance. Some minerals, such as gold, invariably show the same colour, while others can match any colour in the spectrum. Quartz is typical here, ranging from colourless to many coloured varieties, with some, such as amethyst, jasper and citrine; being very well known. More reliable is streak, which is the colour of the powdered mineral, most easily gained in a softer mineral by rubbing it across an unglazed porcelain plate. Many minerals of different hues, such as quartz, give white streaks so that the streak test is useful for only some candidates. Hematite, a dark, metallic iron oxide mineral, is well-known for its red streak.

A mineral can have some special property that makes it instantly recognisable. Magnetite, another dark metallic iron oxide mineral, is strongly magnetic and will attract and hold a magnet or steel objects such as pins or paperclips. Certain minerals contain radioactive elements that emit rays and particles, which can be detected by a Geiger counter. Some minerals emit beautiful, intense colours when they are bathed in ultraviolet light. This property is called fluorescence and is a helpful, although not definitive, property.

See-through and Shine Besides colour and crystal shape, other important visual aspects are transparency and lustre. Transparency is the extent to which a mineral is completely transparent, partly transparent (translucent) or opaque to light. This can vary for many minerals, but transparency and translucency are important in gemstones. The more transparent the mineral, the more easily light travels through its structure. The mineral structure bends the light and in some cases, depending on the crystal system, splits each ray into two or three separate rays. The extent to which each ray is bent can be measured and is called its refractive index. Each ray produces a characteristic colour, so that minerals which transmit light may show up to three colours when viewed from different directions. This is of particular use when gem varieties are cut or polished.

Lustre is the shine of a mineral. Some minerals, like diamond and zircon, are very bright (adamantine) in lustre. Many minerals, including quartz, are glassy (vitreous) in lustre. Others can be pearly, silky, resinous, or just earthy or dull. Many metal-rich minerals show a metallic lustre. Minerals may vary in the strength and nature of their lustre, so it is a useful rather than diagnostic property in mineral recognition.

Measurables: Hardness and Density

Minerals have different resistances to scratching. In 1822, Frederich Mohs, a German mineralogist, devised a comparative hardness scale for minerals and gemstones that is widely used today. At one end of the scale, registering 10, is the hardest natural substance—diamond. At the other end, at 1, is the soft, easily powdered mineral talc. More generally, the density of a mineral compared with the density of water, known as its specific gravity (SG), is a useful test. It can be roughly estimated by judging the size of the specimen relative to its weight, but otherwise an accurate measurement needs to take the weight of the mineral in air and water or to test it against heavy liquids of known density. These are all physical tests and this guide lists some of the measurable physical attributes that can identify minerals.

Planes of Weakness: Cleavage

Cleavage is an obvious property in some minerals and even its absence can aid identification, as with quartz. Cleavage results from planes of weakness running through certain crystal directions of a mineral. Good examples are seen in the mica minerals, where one strong cleavage parallel to the base of the crystal gives this mineral its strongly sheeted appearance. In other minerals, more than one cleavage is present, although they may vary

in strength. In calcite, three sets of strong cleavages readily break up crystals into rhomb-shaped pieces. Cleavage planes need to be distinguished from crystal faces, which are the primary form of the mineral. Minerals can break in a curved, jagged or smooth style. The way they break is known as their fracture.

SCALE OF HARDNESS: MOHS' SCALE

Talc	1
Gypsum	2
Calcite	3
Fluorite	4
Apatite	5
Orthoclase	6
Quartz	7
Topaz	8
Corundum	9
Diamond	10
Fingernail	~ 2.5
Copper coin	~ 3.0
Window glass	~ 5.5
Knife blade	~ 6.0
Steel file	~ 6.5

Variation on a Theme: Habit and Form

Finally, the particular habit of a crystal or form of the mineral needs to be considered. This controls the overall external appearance of a mineral. Minerals can grow in needle-like, tabular or radiating crystal habits or form grape-like, sheaf-like or kidney-like shapes. There is endless variety in crystal and mineral growth, which is part of the challenge of recognising minerals.

Range of Minerals It is hoped that this guide, with its accompanying colour photographs of Australian gemstones and minerals plus the short descriptions of their salient features will provide a resource for identifying minerals. There is no doubt that some minerals can be very difficult to pin down. Visiting museum displays and mineral shows, and consulting books, magazines, journals and online sources greatly helps collectors see the range of possibilities and learn about the rarer mineral types.

Minerals do not form in isolation, even though they may be presented as single objects after collection. They grow in a matrix of other minerals. A great delight in investigating the mineral world, besides the aesthetic pleasure of viewing perfect crystal examples, is seeing minerals in their natural habitat or matrix. Two or more minerals together can provide appealing visual contrasts in a single specimen.

Behind all this lurks the geological history each mineral holds. Minerals have grown throughout Earth's history, under many different chemical conditions. The oldest mineral known is a zircon from Western Australia, dated at well over four billion years. Minerals are still forming at this moment within the Earth and, in time, erosion or human activity will reveal their presence. This is the true heritage of minerals and this modest guide forms but a first step into this wider world.

IDENTIFYING GEMSTONES

Because minerals vary in their chemistry and basic structure, they differ in many other ways as well. They vary in hardness, specific gravity, the way they interact with light, a tendency to cleave along certain directions and many other physical ways. When minerals are transformed into gemstones, all their mineral qualities (called properties) remain intact, forming the basis for a number of identification tests. Gemstones must be distinguished, not only from each other, but also from synthetic equivalents or cheap imitations. Visual examination alone is insufficient, since stones can look very similar in colour and cut yet be quite different materials. It would be perfectly possible to put together a group of about 10 green stones that looked much alike in colour, but were, in fact, emerald, synthetic emerald, glass, tourmaline, garnet, sapphire, chrysoberyl, kornerupine, diopside and zircon! An attractive, green cabochon in a ring could be emerald, jadeite, chrysoprase or dyed chalcedony. Gemstone identification tests involve non-destructive methods, based on optical properties, heat conductivity, density in comparison with water (specific gravity) and internal inclusions. People who are qualified to identify gemstones are called gemmologists.

An important property that varies among gemstones is hardness. Minerals and gemstones are ranked by their resistance to scratching and, looking at the comparative hardness scale, it is obvious that the harder gems (7 and above) are most widely used as gemstones, particularly in rings. This test is useful only for rough material or the base of carvings, as it leaves behind a small scratch. Indeed, for cut stones, there are more efficient identification tests.

Cutting Gemstones: Improving on Nature

A gemstone needs fashioning to bring out its potential beauty. Although it may be attractive as a rough pebble, it will look much more so as a faceted stone, with facet angles precisely positioned to capture light, reflect it off the bottom facets and send it back through the top of the stone to the eye, maximising the impact. A person who cuts gemstones is called a lapidary.

The earliest method of cutting gemstones was to form them into a domed shape, called a cabochon. The material was first ground into the required shape, then polished. This cut is used today for opaque materials (such as turquoise), patterned materials (like tiger's eye or opal), or translucent materials (such as some garnets or lower quality ruby or emerald). The cut requires no particular alignment and the cutter considers only the final, desired appearance. However, with catseye stones, or star stones, alignment is crucial to the effect.

For transparent stones, faceting is preferable. Faceting requires a good knowledge of crystals and their optic properties, since the lapidary must make a number of vital decisions when orienting the stone for cutting. Faceted cuts have become more complex and sophisticated over time, with simple cuts like the table cut and the rose cut giving way to the emerald cut and the brilliant cut. Variations on these classic cuts are many and frequent. A modification of the brilliant cut, called the zircon cut, was developed especially for zircons, increasing their brilliance with extra facets. Experienced lapidaries often create their own individual cuts, within a defined, mathematical framework.

Because diamond has exceptional qualities, diamond cutting is a specialised occupation and particular cuts have been designed for diamond alone. The round brilliant cut with 57 facets was developed, in 1919, to maximise the brilliance and fire (high dispersion) of diamond and has become synonymous with the stone. Modifications have occurred in both shape of cut and number of facets and many diamonds are cut as ovals, marquise shapes, trilliants, pear shapes or hearts, depending on the shape of the original rough.

VALUING GEMSTONES

What are they worth? This is one of the most-asked questions about gemstones. The value of gemstones is twofold. First, they retain a tremendous personal and sentimental value for people of all ages and are used to mark the milestones of life—birth, coming of age, betrothal, marriage, anniversaries and even death. Second, they have a commercial value, which is intimately linked to their beauty and short supply. From earliest times gems have been worn as talismans or symbols of power and prestige. Diamonds were worn mainly by men, however, until the 15th century, when Agnes Sorel, mistress of Charles VII of France, defied convention and flaunted her gifts of sumptuous diamond jewellery in public.

Gemstones are priced for their innate quality, which is assessed by a number of discernible criteria. For instance, if it is a red

COMMON GEMSTONE CUTS

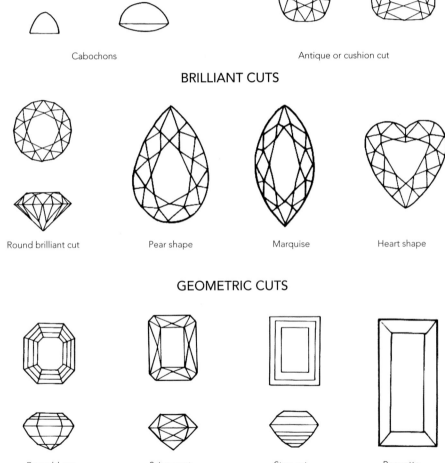

OLDER CUTS

Cabochons

Antique or cushion cut

BRILLIANT CUTS

Round brilliant cut

Pear shape

Marquise

Heart shape

GEOMETRIC CUTS

Emerald cut

Scissor cut

Step cut

Baguette

stone, is it a strong, pure red? Is it a clear stone, free of inclusions, allowing light to travel through it unimpeded? Is the cut well-proportioned, with precisely matching facets? Size and rarity come into the equation. Large rubies, for instance, are very rare in nature and their value will increase exponentially with their size. Smoky quartz, however, is often found in large crystals, so the price increase for a large stone is not great.

The size of gemstones is expressed as a weight, called a carat. The word carat comes from the Greek name for the carob tree, which was common in the Middle East and produced seeds that, when dried, were so uniform in weight they were used as a unit of weight by ancient traders. In our electronic age, a carat is precisely 0.2 grams. Value is assessed by dealers, according to quality, as a price per carat and then multiplied by the number of carats to give the selling price.

A natural, untreated stone is always worth more than a treated stone. Stones may have their colour improved by heating irradiation or electron bombardment and where this is detectible their value is appropriately reduced. A large, golden diamond of 104 carats, named the Deepdene, sold at auction in 1997 for under US$7,000 per carat, after it was revealed that its colour had been enhanced by irradiation followed by heat treatment (annealing). Had it been a naturally vivid yellow stone, its price would have been in the vicinity of around US$60–70,000 per carat. This was a price difference of around US$6,000,000.

Value is directly influenced by rarity, an example being the pink to red diamonds currently produced by the Argyle Diamond Mine in Western Australia. These rare and beautiful diamonds can sell for more than US $1,000,000 per carat, dependent on their colour, size and clarity. The largest faceted pink diamond from Argyle to date is a radiant cut, light pink stone of 4.15 carats.

A vibrant black opal with a unique pattern of strong colours could fetch a similarly high price.

SELLING GEMSTONES

Throughout previous centuries only the powerful and rich were able to buy gemstones. Today, an international mass market has emerged with a seemingly insatiable demand for jewellery stones in calibrated sizes. Exploration for diamonds and other gemstones has increased and new mines are constantly sought to satisfy gemstone lovers.

In the case of diamonds, the market has, in the past, been carefully controlled by an international diamond mining company called De Beers, which oversaw the whole process from mine to buyer and was therefore able to limit the number of diamonds on the market at any one time. This control stabilised the price of diamonds, preventing it from fluctuating with supply and other factors. Today, other large mining companies also produce diamonds. De Beers retains mines in Africa and Canada, sells its rough diamonds through the Diamond Trading Company and markets its own high quality, branded stones through chosen outlets.

Aerial view of the Argyle Diamond Mine, W.A.

FASHION AND GEMSTONES

Gemstones may come in and out of fashion. Because of the present large supply of small, near-gem quality diamonds and their inexpensive cutting in India, diamond-set jewellery has become available and fashionable. Television shopping channels and internet sales have stimulated a fashion for such items, together with other well-known gemstones such as sapphires, amethysts, rubies, emeralds and topaz. Opals have again become internationally popular, after a period of eclipse in the last century. This has been closely related to the discoveries in Australia and the large opal reserves still to be tapped in this country. Supply and fashion are always intimately linked.

Lastly, there are those individuals who prefer to be outside fashion, or perhaps even to lead it.

Faceted diamond (5.15 carats), Argyle Diamond Mine, WA.

24

Such people will choose an unusual gemstone, one that is not often seen on someone else. It may be a fiery, golden-brown sphene (titanite) from the Northern Territory, a rare orange sapphire from the Australian sapphire fields or perhaps a limpid, yellow feldspar from the Hogarth Range in New South Wales.

AUSTRALIAN MINERAL AND GEM RESOURCES

Australia, with its long geological history, includes some of the world's oldest rocks and holds a wide range of minerals and their gem varieties. Some minerals have brought Australia world-wide fame, not just because they form deposits of economic worth, but because they are outstanding examples. Gold is one of these icons because, during Australia's gold rush days, the largest gold nuggets ever found came to light. The biggest of all, the 'Welcome Stranger' nugget, was unearthed in 1863, near

Alluvial gold workings, Moliagul, Vic.

Moliagul, Victoria, weighing around 2,285 troy ounces of gold, which is just over 71 kg. Broken Hill in outback New South Wales also attracted world attention for the beauty and variety of the alteration minerals found in the weathered cap of the ore body. A specimen of cerussite, a lead carbonate mineral, has featured among the world's finest mineral specimens. In 1985 it was depicted on an Australia Post pre-stamped envelope to celebrate the centenary of mining at Broken Hill. One of the famous minerals is crocoite, a lead chromate mineral. Nearly every mineral collection around the world boasts a crocoite specimen and the best crocoite ever found comes from Dundas in Tasmania. Its bright, orange-red,

Unearthing the Welcome Stranger Nugget.

What are Gemstones & Minerals?

Crocoite mine, Dundas, Tas.

shining and elongated crystals make it one of the most attractive of all minerals.

Australian gemstones also include some world-beaters. The most renowned is probably the kaleidoscopic coloured precious opal. The Australian opal fields are unrivalled for their quality, quantity and range of stones. Some of the most spectacular specimens receive names that speak of their glory, such as Red Admiral, Fire of Andamooka, Halleys Comet, Desert Rain and the Galaxy. The lives, wins and losses of fortunes, as well as the personalities of the characters involved in mining opal form part of the folklore of outback Australia. Sapphires are also a superstar gemstone, but unfortunately their illustrious nature has been dimmed by Australian stones being sold overseas as Thai sapphires. Several large, dark Australian sapphires have been carved into heads of US presidents. Diamonds from Australia also dazzled the world markets after the Argyle Mine began production in the Kimberley region of Western Australia in 1985. A small but steady stream of pink to red diamonds appeared among the diamond stocks, commanding the world supply of such stones and fetching prices in excess of a million Australian dollars for

Crocoite, Dundas, Tas.

Opal miner, Lightning Ridge area, NSW.

top coloured stones. Less flamboyant but still unique in their way, were the diamonds mined in northern New South Wales since the late 1800s. They are an unusual type of diamond and the original parent rock is yet to be found.

The Science Side Australian minerals and gemstones have made their mark in the mineral world, but new discoveries still await. Some discoveries have been made by professional mineralogists, others by amateurs and collectors who take specimens to institutions such as universities and museums for further investigation. Sometimes, identification of a mineral defies simple tests but with our

Aerial view of Broken Hill, NSW.

Cerussite (33x26cm), Broken Hill, NSW.

modern technology, such as X-ray methods and electron, ion or laser beam chemical analyses at mineralogical laboratories, even the hardest cases usually yield their secrets.

Concentrations of valuable minerals in ore bodies receive much scientific study because of their economic importance. These studies deal with two types of mineral associations in the ore bodies. The primary mineral deposit represents the pristine mineralogy, while the secondary minerals that formed from this grow in a zone of alteration due to atmospheric interaction. Many primary ores contain sulfide minerals (metal combined with sulfur) or sulfosalt minerals (a wider range of metals combined with sulfur). These minerals alter as groundwaters with dissolved oxygen and carbon dioxide react with

Faceted sapphires (largest stone over 12 carats) eastern Australia.

them and release their metals. This forms a wide range of oxygen-rich secondary minerals.

Over 200 minerals have been discovered and named for the first time in Australia. Such specimens are known as type specimens, because they form important reference material to settle later mineral identification: A number of minerals thought to be new have subsequently proved to be invalid. Australian type minerals have been named either for an aspect of their nature, after their place of origin or for prominent mineral identities or researchers.

Additional finds of minerals and gemstones and even of minerals that are new to science continue to emerge in Australia. A burst in new mineral species described from Australia has taken place since the 1960s. This is largely due to improved technology, expansion in mineral collecting and a boom in locating mineral deposits. Interaction between amateur and professional mineralogists has played an important role in this and it is hoped this guide will further this relationship.

Sapphire mine, New England district, NSW.

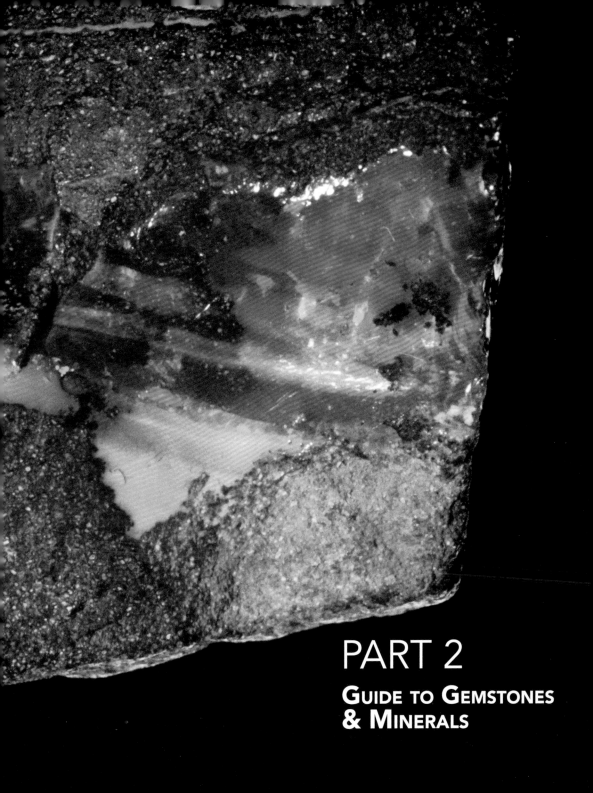

PART 2

GUIDE TO GEMSTONES & MINERALS

Diamond

Diamonds originate in the Earth's mantle. They are usually transported to the surface in volcanic pipes of kimberlite or lamproite rock. From these, they wash into rivers and often finish up in alluvial deposits far from their source. However, some eastern Australian diamonds are unusual and may come from a source other than the typical kimberlite or lamproite.

Diamond is an outstanding natural material. Its hardness, high lustre, fire (high dispersion) and clarity make it unique. Western Australia's Argyle Mine in north Western Australia has produced a huge volume of diamonds, while

fields at Ellendale, north Western Australia, Merlin, Northern Territory, and Copeton, New South Wales, have produced different types of stones.

Diamond is composed of only one element—carbon. Its favoured crystal shape is an octahedron but often other crystal forms prevail as a result of growth conditions. Because of their high (adamantine) lustre, diamond crystals are usually very bright and tend to stand out from accompanying minerals in a fossicker's pan.

• *Diamond deposits*

Yellow diamond crystal, 11.47 ct, Ellendale, WA.

ARGYLE DIAMONDS

Crystals from the Argyle mine are usually slightly rounded (resorbed) in shape as a result of magmatic corrosion during transport to the surface. Only about five per cent of the diamonds mined are gem quality, with the remainder being used for industrial purposes.

Argyle diamond concentrate.

30

ARGYLE COLOURS

Diamonds occur in a wide range of colours—from colourless to grey, yellow, brown, orange, green, blue, pink, red and intermediate colours. These colours are caused by chemical impurities like nitrogen, boron and hydrogen, and/or crystal growth defects. The most valuable diamonds are those with no colour at all or those with an attractive, distinct colour, which are called 'fancies'. Argyle diamonds are predominantly shades of yellow and brown. In contrast, Ellendale yields fancy yellow stones.

Stones from the Argyle Pink Diamonds Tender, 2013.

Colour range of Argyle diamond crystals.

ARGYLE PINKS

Each year, a tiny percentage of Argyle's production is pink, currently the world's only dependable supply of these rare diamonds. Colours range from various shades of pink to red. These colours are caused by deformation of the crystal lattice.

COPETON DIAMONDS

Diamond crystals from around Copeton and Bingara, in the New England area of New South Wales, look different to other Australian diamonds. They usually fall into two colour groups—bright yellow and white (colourless). They are often very lustrous and are octahedral or rounded forms.

Copeton diamond crystals.

Faceted Copeton diamonds.

LARGE DIAMONDS

Australia's largest diamond (104.73 carats) came from a Merlin, Northern Territory, kimberlite pipe and was cut into one large stone and a number of smaller ones. A large 12.76 ct. pink diamond crystal from Argyle, not suitable for faceting, was donated to the Museum of Victoria.

DIAMOND NOTES

Chemistry:	Carbon
Crystal system:	Cubic
Hardness:	10
Refractive index:	2.417
Specific gravity:	3.52
Dispersion:	High (0.044)
Cleavage:	Perfect
Lustre:	Adamantine

Australia's largest diamond crystal, before cutting.

BLUE SAPPHIRE

Sapphire and ruby are the two gem varieties of the mineral corundum, an aluminium oxide. This mineral is coloured by additional trace elements in its structure. Sapphire is the name used for all colours of gem corundum other than red, which is called ruby.

Sapphires are widely distributed throughout eastern Australia. They wash

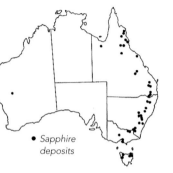

Sapphire deposits

out of basaltic volcanic rocks, particularly those formed in explosive deposits. Formed in deep igneous or metamorphic rocks, they have been randomly plucked and carried to the

Sapphire crystal in basalt.

surface by basalt. Two types of sapphire come from these basaltic sources. Most common are blue, green and yellow colour-zoned sapphires of an igneous origin. More unusual is a range of fancy-coloured, weakly zoned sapphires with a metamorphic origin. In other parts of Australia, sapphires are rare and are generally found in metamorphic host rocks.

SAPPHIRE CRYSTALS

Sapphire crystals are often barrel-shaped or elongated bipyramids. These may break at the middle into a dog-tooth shape. Crystal exteriors often have a corroded appearance, caused by magma during their passage to the surface, or are rounded and worn due to alluvial transport.

Sapphire crystals.

COLOUR-ZONING

Hexagonal colour zoning is a growth feature, often very pronounced in Australian sapphires. Crystals may be banded in several colours, or show dark and light zones of one colour. Sapphires are also strongly dichroic, that is they show two differing colours when viewed from different crystal directions. A sapphire may look green from one side and blue from another.

Colour-zoned sapphire crystal.

33

FACETED SAPPHIRE

Blue sapphires are the most popular. The rich blue of a fine sapphire is caused by traces of iron and titanium. Colour is enhanced by cutting the stone with its table (top) at right angles to the vertical crystal axis, so that a strong blue, undiluted by green, is presented to the eye. The New England area in New South Wales produces most of Australia's blue sapphires.

Faceted sapphire, New England, NSW.

SAPPHIRE NOTES

Chemistry:	Aluminium oxide
Crystal system:	Trigonal
Hardness:	9
Refractive index:	1.76–1.78
Specific gravity:	3.90–4.00
Dispersion:	Moderate (0.018)
Cleavage:	None
Lustre:	Vitreous

CARVED SAPPHIRE

Material that is not suitable for faceting may be carved. Some very large Australian sapphires have been made into carvings, such as the famous series of portraits of four past US Presidents—Lincoln, Washington, Jefferson and Eisenhower.

Carved sapphire.

SAPPHIRE INCLUSIONS

Sapphires often contain fluid or mineral inclusions, which are remnants of their geological origin. Inclusions of radioactive minerals, such as zircon, can be dated to give an age of formation for the enclosing sapphire, assisting geological research and exploration.

Zircon inclusion in sapphire (magnified).

FANCY-COLOURED SAPPHIRE

Besides blue, sapphires occur in a wide range of colours. They can be colourless, pink, lavender, purple, orange, yellow, green or particoloured. These fancy-coloured stones are described as sapphire, preceded by the colour, as in 'green sapphire'. Australian yellow sapphires are thought to be coloured by the presence of highly oxidised iron, while other colours may be caused by various combinations of titanium, iron, nickel and chromium.

Sapphire colour range: faceted stones.

LARGE SAPPHIRES

Sapphire crystals can grow to large sizes. The Kingsley Sapphire (162 carats) was originally part of a larger crystal. Like many of the larger sapphires, it was found near Rubyvale, on the central Queensland sapphire fields. It is a spectacular green and yellow, parti-coloured stone. Another large sapphire was the Centenary Sapphire (2,020 carats), a yellow and blue, parti-coloured stone. Such large sapphires may be cut or remain in collections as examples of fine, natural material.

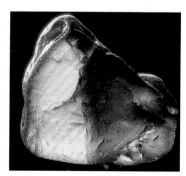

'Kingsley sapphire', a 162-carat crystal.

YELLOW AND GREEN SAPPHIRE

Green and yellow stones are commonly found on the Australian sapphire fields. Greens occur in a number of shades and yellows vary from greenish yellow to intense yellow or deep gold. Top quality green, yellow or gold sapphires weighing over a carat, however, are rare. The Anakie field in central Queensland is reputed to produce the finest yellow and green stones.

Faceted golden sapphire.

ORANGE SAPPHIRE

Bright orange sapphires are particularly uncommon on the sapphire fields. Their colour is thought to result from traces of iron and nickel with some chromium. This rare stone came from the private collection of a mine owner.

Faceted orange sapphire.

STAR SAPPHIRE

When 'silk' is thickly distributed throughout the sapphire, stones can be cut into cabochons that reflect light from the oriented inclusions in the form of six-rayed, or sometimes 12-rayed, stars. Star sapphires are found in a variety of colours but black star sapphires are the most common in Australia.

Star Sapphire.

COLOUR-CHANGE SAPPHIRE

From time to time sapphires are found that appear as different colours under daylight and artificial light. These stones are said to possess a 'colour change'. Lights of different wavelengths are absorbed differently by the stone, causing a variation in the emergent colours. The large sapphire pictured is reddish brown under electric tungsten light and brownish green in daylight. It also shows a broad band of oriented, needle-like crystals of an included mineral, referred to as 'silk', across its table.

Faceted colour-change sapphire.

RUBY

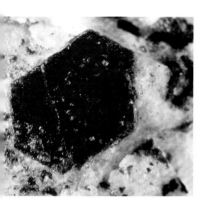

Ruby crystal in feldspar-rich gneiss.

Ruby and sapphire are gem varieties of the mineral, corundum. Ruby deposits, however, are rarer than sapphire deposits because they are dependent on the presence of the element, chromium. Chromium gives ruby its red colour, with modification from iron, titanium and vanadium. Ruby is usually found in metamorphic rocks, such as those in the Harts Range, Northern Territory. However, a more transparent, gem-quality ruby comes from a few basaltic terrains in eastern Australia, where it was brought up from underlying metamorphic sources by volcanic action. Rubies are mainly found in the Barrington–Gloucester area but also occur in the Macquarie River and Tumbarumba alluvials, New South Wales. They are associated with fancy coloured sapphires and they shed together into surrounding alluvial deposits. Very occasionally rubies are found on the New England sapphire fields.

Ruby deposits

HARTS RANGE RUBY

Ruby tends to form smaller, more tabular crystals than sapphire. Ruby from the Harts Range is an attractive rosy colour and is opaque. Hexagonal crystals occur in a light-coloured, feldspathic gneiss and are used for cabochons, carvings and as specimens.

FACETING-QUALITY RUBY

Transparent, faceting-quality rubies are found in the area around Barrington and Gloucester Tops, New South Wales. Here, more than in any other eastern Australian locality, rubies occur in an equal distribution with sapphires. Crystals are small (from 2–6 mm) and vary from light to deep red.

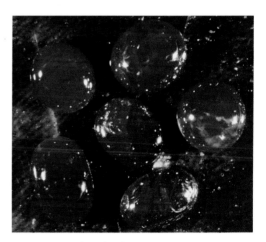

Harts Range ruby cabochons.

Faceting-quality ruby crystals.

Ruby–sapphire suite: crystals.

RUBY CUTTING

Unlike sapphires, large rubies are rare. However, attractive rubies of over a carat have been cut from material from Barrington and Gloucester Tops. The material contains some mineral and fluid inclusions but is relatively clear. To obtain the best colour, a ruby is generally cut with its table perpendicular to the vertical crystal axis. This displays only its purplish red colour, without interference from the orange colour present in other crystal directions.

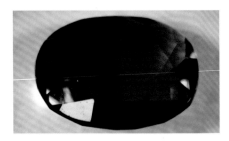

Faceted ruby.

RUBY–SAPPHIRE SUITE

The Barrington Tops rubies grade into related pink, purple and mauve sapphires which, in turn, grade into blue stones. These ruby associates are distinct from the more prevalent blue, green and yellow, strongly colour-zoned types.

EAST COAST RUBY

Australian east coast deposits of ruby are not well-known internationally. Nevertheless these deposits have produced bright gemstones of good colour. The colour of ruby is further enhanced by its strong, red fluorescence in response to ultraviolet light.

Gloucester rubies set in ring with Copeton diamonds.

RUBY NOTES

Chemistry:	Aluminium oxide
Crystal system:	Trigonal
Hardness:	9
Refractive index:	1.76–1.78
Specific gravity:	3.90–4.00
Dispersion:	Moderate (0.018)
Cleavage:	None
Lustre:	Vitreous

PRECIOUS OPAL

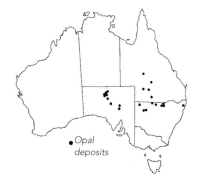

● *Opal deposits*

Opal is a common mineral, a hardened compound of silica and water, and it occurs in many countries. Precious opal, however, with its bright play of colour, is considerably rarer. The term 'play of colour' describes the effect, unique to opal, of spectral colours passing over and through the stone as it is moved. In Australia, precious opal is found mainly in sandstones and mudstones that were deeply weathered under unusual climatic conditions. This weathering released silica into groundwaters, where it slowly condensed into a hardened gel and settled into the layers of submicroscopic spheres, which cause its unique colour play. A large area of central Australia, once an inland sea, is a happy hunting ground for opal. Australia supplies around 95 per cent of the world's precious opal from large deposits in New South Wales, South Australia and Queensland.

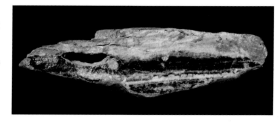

Opal seam.

OPAL COLOUR

The colours of precious opal result from its unusual structure, which breaks white light into its spectral colours. Colours change with the angle of incidence of light, as the opal moves. The endless variety of colour 'patterns' ensures that no two opals are exactly alike.

Black opal.

BLACK OPAL

The body tone of precious opal varies, ranging from white to light to dark to black. Others have a distinct gold or brown body colour. Black opal with a full spectrum of colours is most prized. Lightning Ridge produces most of the world's black opal.

Black opal in ring.

39

LIGHT OPAL

Light opal has a light-coloured or white background to the play of colour. South Australia is renowned for its fine, light opal, although other types also occur. All other factors being equal, light or white opal is not as highly priced as dark or black opal. Opal is cut in a cabochon shape to maximise the play of colour effect.

Light opal.

CRYSTAL OPAL

Precious opal that is semi-transparent or transparent is called crystal opal. This is a very attractive type, with play of colour visible inside, as well as outside, the opal. Sometimes the body colour has a yellow or brown tinge.

Crystal opal, with yellow body colour.

OPAL CARVINGS

Some precious opal is interspersed with an opaque grey opal called 'potch'. This base material can be carved into designs that accentuate colourful highlights.

Opal cameo.

OPAL NOTES

Chemistry:	Hydrated silica
Crystal system:	Amorphous or containing crystals of crystabolite and/or tridymite.
Hardness:	5–6.5
Refractive index:	1.43–1.47
Specific gravity:	1.93–2.20
Lustre:	Resinous to vitreous

BOULDER OPAL

Australia produces another type of precious opal called boulder opal, which is a thin layer of richly coloured opal, inseparable from its host rock. The two are cut together and often given a free-form shape with a naturally undulating surface.

Boulder opal is found mostly in Queensland. Like solid opal, it originates in sedimentary rocks. In this case, however, the deep weathering that concentrated silica in groundwater also mobilised considerable iron, forming ironstone layers, which acted as a support for later opal deposits. Opal subsequently formed within ironstone concretions and as seams or pipes in ironstone.

Boulder opal on matrix.

YOWAH NUTS

Yowah nuts are formed when opal has filled the cracks and cavities in the surrounding ironstone. Small, spherical ironstone concretions, partly filled with opal, weather out of softer surrounding rock. They are plentiful on the Yowah opal field in Queensland.

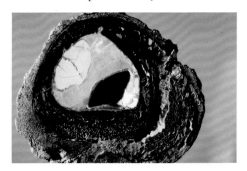

Sliced Yowah 'nut'.

BOULDER OPAL IN MATRIX

Boulder opal is intimately associated with its ironstone matrix, segments of which are sometimes visible in the opal's interior. Ironstone containing many tiny veins and pools of precious opal can itself be polished to highlight these inclusions. This attractive but lower-priced material is called matrix opal. As boulder opal is moved about in the hand, the colour flashes regroup, forming a kaleidescope of different colour patterns. Red is seen at some angles, only to be replaced by blue or green at different angles.

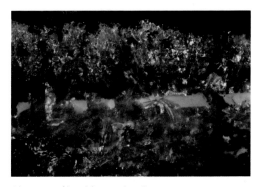

Close-up of boulder opal and matrix.

41

Boulder opal showing blue flashes.

The same opal showing red flashes.

EXCEPTIONAL OPALS

Sometimes very large pieces of boulder opal are found. These may be revealed as broad 'sheets' of colour when ironstone boulders are split open. The rock is trimmed around the area of opal and the surface can be polished to maximise the brilliant colour. Sometimes colour will appear on several sides of these large specimens. Exceptional stones are often given names, such as the 'Mariora Star' and the 'Galaxy Opal'.

'Galaxy Opal'.

DESCRIBING OPAL

Opal was declared Australia's National gemstone in 1993 and black opal became the New South Wales State gemstone in 2011. Because of the large number of popular names for different types of opal, it became necessary to standardize opal terminology. There are two types of opal: precious opal, with a 'play of colour' and common opal (sometimes called 'potch'), with none.

Precious Opal

There are three types of precious opal:

- Solid opal, which is opal throughout the stone.
- Boulder opal, which is inseparable from its backing of host rock, or matrix.
- Matrix opal, which is opal distributed in small veins and pores throughout the matrix and polished in one piece with it.

Background colour Precious opal is described by its background colour (body tone) and transparency.

- Light to white opal has a light-coloured body tone.
- Dark to black opal has a dark to very dark (black) body tone.
- Crystal opal is semi-transparent or transparent.

Composites Inexpensive gemstones are made by cementing thin slices of precious opal to other materials.

- Doublets (two pieces): opal backed by another material.
- Triplets (three pieces): a slice of opal, a backing and a transparent top layer.
- Mosaic and chip opals: small pieces of opal on a base or in resin.

OTHER OPAL

Precious opal can be found in any geological environment. It is sometimes found in volcanic rocks in eastern Australia, where it settled into cavities and cracks left after the lava cooled. It has even

been found in metamorphic rock near Coolgardie in Western Australia. At Tintenbar in New South Wales, heated groundwaters dissolved silica from underlying diatomite (a silica-rich rock) before rising to fill cracks and cavities in the lava flow. These opals have a good play of colour but the colours tend to be paler and more diffuse than in sedimentary opal. Volcanic opal is generally less stable than that formed in a settled, sedimentary environment and may crack on exposure to the air.

Volcanic opal.

HYALITE OPAL

Another type of opal formed in volcanic rocks is hyalite. Hyalite is colourless to bluish and transparent and has no colour play. Examples resemble small, glassy globules piled onto the matrix.

Green common opal.

Hyalite opal.

COMMON OPAL

Common opal is often found in and around volcanic rocks. It is generally grey or brown but can occur in attractive colours. Bright green 'prase opal' is coloured by traces of nickel minerals and can resemble chrysoprase. 'Honey opal' is a warm golden brown and may be opaque or transparent. 'Moss opal', sometimes transparent, contains dendritic mineral inclusions resembling fern fronds or moss.

43

OPAL REPLACEMENTS

Sometimes opal has filled the spaces left in a sedimentary environment by shells, bones, vegetation or even other minerals that had been dissolved by changes in surrounding conditions. These are actually fossil casts, since they are replacements of the original material, and sometimes reproduce minute, structural detail. The opal may be either precious or common opal. Opalised wood is often found, sometimes with veins of precious opal.

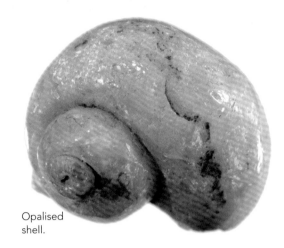

Opalised shell.

Common opal replacement of wood.

MARINE FOSSILS

Opal replacements of shells and marine creatures are often found on the opal fields. These can be as large and complete as a pliosaur or as small as a snail. A well-known example is 'Eric' the pliosaur, on display at the Australian Museum in Sydney. In the past, many precious opal 'fossils' were cut into cabochons for jewellery but increasingly they are preserved as specimens, retaining their value as both opal and fossil.

OPAL 'PINEAPPLES'

Unusual spiky crystal clusters, resembling pineapples, have been given the name 'opal pineapples'. These are opal replacements (pseudomorphs) of an earlier mineral, ikaite, which has decomposed due to a change in its environment. The opal varies from common to precious. Opal pineapples are found only at White Cliffs, New South Wales.

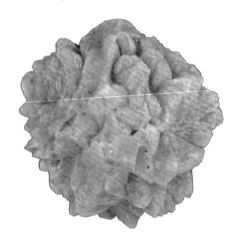

Opal 'pineapple'.

CRYSTALLISED QUARTZ

Quartz is Earth's most common mineral. A silicon dioxide, it is an essential mineral in granitic and pegmatitic rocks, where it

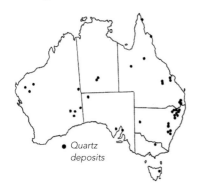

● Quartz
  deposits

forms large crystals. It is abundant in metamorphic rocks, such as quartzites, schists and gneisses, in ore bodies and the veins lacing a wide range of rocks. Worn fragments of this resistant mineral are found in sedimentary rocks, such as conglomerates and sandstones, and they also occur in loose sediments.

Quartz crystals.

Formed in such a variety of environments, quartz occurs in many sizes, types and colours.

ROCK CRYSTAL

Colourless, clear quartz is called rock crystal. Because of its purity and coldness, the ancient Greeks thought it was ice so deeply frozen it could never melt. Given sufficient space and solution, colourless quartz crystals can grow very large and crystals over 3 metres long have been found at Kingsgate, New South Wales. Repeated silica solutions can produce one generation of quartz crystals on top of another.

Faceted rock crystal.

FACETED ROCK CRYSTAL

Large, clear gemstones can be cut from rock crystal. The Museum of Victoria holds one of the world's largest faceted rock crystals, a stone of 8,510 carats, from near Bonnie Doon in Victoria. Because the dispersion of quartz is low, rock crystal is not a fiery gem, but its moderate hardness enables it to take a good polish and withstand reasonable wear.

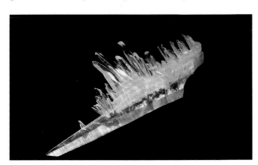

Rock crystal: two generations.

SMOKY QUARTZ

Colourless quartz is a comparatively pure mineral but it does contain traces of some other elements, mainly aluminium. This element causes colourless quartz to become smoky brown if exposed to radiation from surrounding rocks. When very dark and opaque it is called morion. Like the colourless variety, it can grow into large, transparent crystals.

Smoky quartz crystals.

FACETED SMOKY QUARTZ

Smoky quartz, like rock crystal, can provide large, transparent gemstones, ranging from light to dark brown. Smoky quartz is plentiful Australia-wide, with the New England area of New South Wales producing much fine material. However, much of the smoky quartz used in jewellery today is colourless quartz that has been artificially irradiated.

Faceted smoky quartz.

Rutilated quartz cabochons.

INCLUSIONS

Quartz crystals can contain a great variety of other minerals as inclusions. These smaller crystals were enveloped by the larger crystal as it grew. Two minerals frequently found in quartz are rutile and tourmaline. Quartz containing needle-like, golden or bronze crystals of rutile is called rutilated quartz, which is a popular gemstone.

QUARTZ NOTES

Chemistry:	Silicon dioxide
Crystal system:	Trigonal
Hardness:	7
Refractive index:	1.544–1.553
Specific gravity:	2.6
Dispersion:	Low (0.013)
Cleavage:	None
Lustre:	Vitreous

COLOURED QUARTZ

Coloured varieties of quartz occur in similar geological settings to rock crystal and smoky quartz. Their colours come from trace elements in their formative environments or from later geological heating processes. Purple quartz is called amethyst and yellow quartz is known as citrine. Orange-brown quartz is sometimes called 'cairngorm' after the Cairngorm Mountains in Scotland where it was once found. Much amethyst is found in crystals lining hollow cavities (geodes) in volcanic rocks. Unlike rock crystal and smoky quartz, these pointed crystals generally have no prism and display only their rhombohedral terminations. The colour of amethyst ranges from almost colourless to deep purple, with crystals often more deeply coloured at the tip.

Amethyst crystal group.

Amethyst sceptres on smoky quartz.

AMETHYST CRYSTALS
Amethyst crystals generally display strong colour zoning, representing changes in the composition of their growth solutions. This zoning is also apparent in cut stones. Sometimes amethyst forms the termination of a colourless or smoky crystal, creating a picturesque effect. These 'combination' crystals are called amethyst sceptres. A change in the geological environment that formed the prism caused a change in the colour and size of the termination.

AMETHYST
Amethyst, like smoky quartz, owes its colour to a trace element (iron) in combination with natural radiation from its host rocks. It is the most valuable of the quartz gemstones, with rich purple stones being the most prized. Opaque material is carved into cabochons, beads or decorative

Faceted amethyst.

47

Gemstones

objects. Amethyst is found in a number of Australian localities, mainly the New England to Stanthorpe area, Beechworth in Victoria, the Broken Hill area in outback New South Wales, the Mt Isa area in outback Queensland and the Ashburton River area in Western Australia.

CITRINE

Faceted citrine.

Citrine ranges from a very pale yellow to an intense golden colour, sometimes grading into orange or brownish shades. The colour is usually caused by ferric iron. Because citrine and smoky quartz have a colour range similar to the more valuable topaz, they are sometimes wrongly given names containing the word 'topaz', such as

'citrine topaz' or 'smoky topaz'. Citrine has been found in the New England-Stanthorpe area, at Kingsgate, New South Wales, and Beechworth in Victoria. It is not common, however, and most citrine used in jewellery today is obtained by heat-treating amethyst.

OTHER COLOURS

Other colours may be found in quartz. A light green shade of transparent quartz has been produced by heat-treating Brazilian material and is called 'prasiolite'. Rose quartz occurs in light to deep shades of rosy pink. It is usually found in massive form and may be transparent to opaque. Although it has been reported in Australia, no high quality material is produced here. Quartz is plentiful and only the clearest and best quartz is faceted into gemstones. Lesser quality material is used for making cabochons, beads or carvings. Quartz crystals occur in a great number of shapes and sizes, varying from the very tiny crystals that line geodes to large, well-formed prisms. Whether displayed singly or in groups, quartz crystals make popular and attractive mineral specimens.

Quartz crystals and faceted stones.

Faceted citrine and cairngorm.

48

FINE-GRAINED QUARTZ

Chalcedony.

As well as large crystals, quartz forms crystals invisible to the unaided eye. This fine-grained quartz is known as a 'microcrystalline' because the crystals can be seen only under magnification. Chalcedony is the general name for a type of fine-grained quartz with a dense structure of interlocking, fibrous crystals and some hydrous silica. In its purer form, chalcedony is a translucent, white, grey or bluish material with a waxy lustre. However, its aggregate structure can accept a comparatively high percentage of impurities and these have created a number of strongly coloured gem materials. Physical properties, including hardness, are slightly lower than for crystallised quartz but, with its tightly meshed structure, chalcedony is durable and tough.

AGATE

Banded chalcedony is called agate. Agate is usually found in volcanic rocks, in seams filling fractures or in cavities left by gas bubbles. Silica is deposited by a series of siliceous liquids, which partly or completely fill these spaces. Bands are wavy, straight or concentric and can be many different colours, depending on the available colouring agents. Later, these fillings (nodules) weather out of the softer, parent rock.

AGATE PATTERNS

Agates occur in limitless combinations of colour and pattern, making each specimen unique. Sometimes agates stimulate us to imagine landscapes or pictures, such as two samples from Tasmania, the 'Map of Tasmania' agate (see Introduction) and the blue 'Whale'. Because chalcedony is porous, it is often artificially stained for a more colourful effect.

Sliced agate nodules.

49

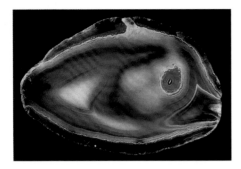

Polished 'Whale' agate.

CHRYSOPRASE

Chrysoprase is a bright green variety of chalcedony, the colour being created by a nickel mineral. It is translucent and can vary from yellow-green to blue-green. The best material is cut into beads and cabochons for jewellery, with lesser quality material carved into decorative objects. Large deposits of high-quality chrysoprase are mined at Marlborough in Queensland.

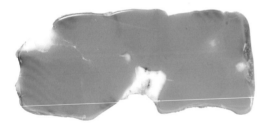

Chrysoprase: polished slice.

JASPER

Jasper is another striking type of fine-grained quartz, with a granular structure. It is opaque and brightly coloured in reds, yellows and greens by iron oxide mineral impurities. It is often given names that describe its many patterns and is used as an ornamental material.

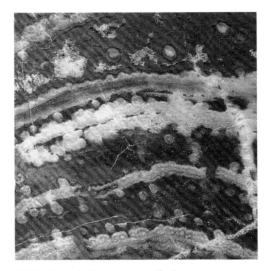

Polished banded jasper (magnified).

SILICIFIED WOOD

Silicified wood is a very attractive material. It was formed when silica in solution had permeated buried wood, replacing the cellular structure, atom by atom, until eventually the wood was entirely replaced by silica. Because of the gradualness of the process, the original woodgrain, and often the cellular structure, has been retained.

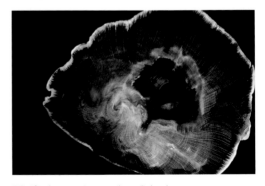

Silicified casuarina trunk, polished.

50

COMPOSITE QUARTZ

Quartz often forms two phases—a microcrystalline and a crystallised phase—in close proximity, as in many agate nodules and thunder eggs. Fine-grained quartz is also found interspersed with other minerals in banded rocks that are attractive and durable enough to be used as ornamentals.

Eastern Australia is well endowed with volcanic rocks bearing agate and quartz infillings. Western Australia is noted for fine tiger's eye, tiger iron and jaspilite from its ancient banded ironstone formations. Thunder eggs occur in spherical masses of a silica-rich volcanic rock called rhyolite. The exterior or 'shell' of the 'egg' is rhyolite and the interior cavity is often star-shaped, due to expansion of gases in the rock before it was filled with siliceous liquids. Infillings of microcrystalline chalcedony or agate are often surmounted by a later growth of crystals.

Thunder egg, sliced.

GEODES

Quartz geodes fill cavities in volcanic rocks with low silica content, like basalt. As well as layers of chalcedony and agate, well-shaped crystals are often found projecting into the cavity, sometimes completely filling the space. Crystals may be colourless, amethyst or smoky quartz.

JASPILITE

Jaspilite is a metamorphic rock, and is well-known from the misnamed Marble Bar in Western Australia. It consists of light-coloured chalcedony bands alternating with bands of dense, fine-grained black or red iron oxides, such as hematite and magnetite. It takes a good polish and is a durable ornamental material.

Quartz geode.

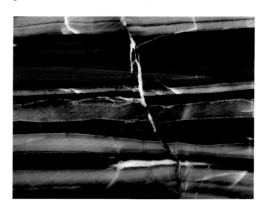

Polished jaspilite (magnified).

TIGER'S EYE

Tiger's eye is an attractive ornamental material from the Pilbara region of Western Australia. Its fibrous structure is due to parallel intergrowth of quartz and blue riebeckite, an amphibole mineral. The resultant shimmering effect (chatoyancy) is enhanced by polishing and cutting. Tiger's eye is usually golden brown, due to oxidation of iron at the surface, but if this does not occur the original, deep blue colour remains. It is often dyed for use in jewellery.

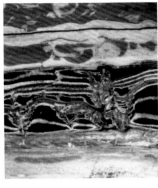

Polished tiger iron (magnified).

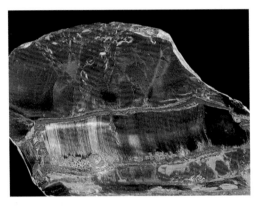

Polished tiger's eye.

TIGER IRON

Tiger iron is the name given to an attractive, metamorphic rock, similar to jaspilite but with the addition of bands of golden tiger's eye. It can be polished and used as an ornamental material.

SILICIOPHITE

Siliciophite, or silicified chrysotile, is another attractive material from the Pilbara area involving former asbestos veins. It is formed from greenish silica that has replaced light-coloured chrysotile asbestos fibres in an altered serpentine rock.

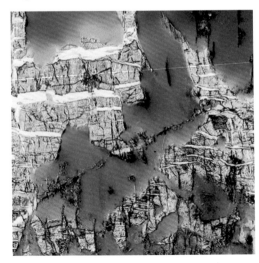

Polished siliciophite (magnified).

EMERALD AND OTHER BERYL

Beryl deposits

Emerald is one of the gem varieties of the mineral beryl. Pure beryl is colourless and its range of beautiful colours is caused by chemical impurities. Each colour is given a varietal name. Emerald is the most valuable but other varieties are highly sought after—blue aquamarine, pink morganite, golden heliodor and the rare red beryl.

Beryl, including some emerald, is typically found as late stage crystallisation in granitic and pegmatitic rocks. These are common throughout Australia, particularly around the New England region of New South Wales, which produces emerald, aquamarine, heliodor and light green beryl, and Mt Surprise in Queensland, which produces aquamarine. In Western Australia, emeralds have been mined around Poona and Menzies, from metamorphic rocks where there has been an interaction between pegmatites and the surrounding mica schists.

Emerald crystal in schist.

EMERALD

The intense green of emerald is caused by traces of chromium and, sometimes, vanadium. Flawless stones are almost unknown and emeralds contain fluid and mineral inclusions. Their value lies in their fine colour rather than their clarity. Because emeralds have a tendency to brittleness, a special cut, known as the 'emerald cut' was devised for them. A rectangular shape emphasises the stone's body colour, while removal of corners protects it against knocks.

Faceted emerald.

EMERALD-ZONED BERYL

Some unusual crystals from Torrington in New South Wales show colour zoning to an extreme degree. They are predominantly clear, colourless beryl, alternating with thin bands of emerald. Stones may be cut at right angles to the prism, producing a standard emerald, or parallel to the prism, producing an unusual striped stone.

Emerald-zoned crystal and faceted stone.

GREEN BERYL

Light green beryl, coloured by iron, can make an attractive gemstone but is called green beryl, not emerald. Green beryl crystals are found as accessory minerals in many of the mines in New England. Large gemstones have been cut from this material, which sometimes contain fluid inclusions.

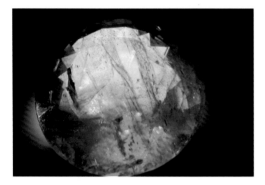

Faceted green beryl.

AQUAMARINE

Aquamarine is a highly prized blue or greenish blue beryl, coloured by iron. It is fairly free of inclusions and large crystals can produce sizeable gemstones. Much aquamarine used in

Aquamarine crystal and faceted stone.

jewellery is yellow-green beryl that has been heat treated until it turns blue.

GOLDEN BERYL

Like aquamarine, golden beryl (heliodor) owes its colour to traces of iron. While uncommon in Australia, slim yellow crystals have been found in the New England area, particularly around Torrington.

Golden beryl crystal.

BERYL NOTES

Chemistry:	Beryllium aluminium oxide
Crystal system:	Hexagonal
Hardness:	7.5
Refractive index:	1.565–1.590
Specific gravity:	2.68–2.90
Dispersion:	Low (0.014)
Lustre:	Vitreous

TOPAZ

● Topaz
deposits

Topaz may be colourless or blue, pink, red, yellow, orange or brown. Although the hardest of the silicate minerals, it has a strong tendency to cleave in a direction parallel to its crystal base. This perfect cleavage makes skilful cutting essential. Topaz also needs protection against knocks or falls.

Topaz crystals have vertical striations along the length of their prism. When these are visible, they provide an easy way to distinguish topaz crystals from similar-looking quartz, which has horizontal striations. Topaz is quite common in Australian granite and pegmatite rocks, particularly in late stage, tin-mineralised veins, called greisens. It also appears in contact metamorphosed zones and, because of its hardness, is found as a heavy mineral in alluvial deposits.

Topaz crystal on matrix.

TOPAZ

Australia produces fine, gem topaz from several localities, mainly Oban in New South Wales, Mt Surprise in Queensland and Flinders Island off Tasmania. Most Australian material is colourless or light blue. Colour zoning from colourless to light blue or pinkish brown, is often present.

Blue-zoned topaz crystal.

BLUE TOPAZ

The light blue colour of natural topaz is caused by gaps in the structure (colour centres), which are an effect of natural radiation. These colour centres alter colour absorption and transmission by the material. Large quantities of bright blue topaz are produced for the jewellery market by artificially irradiating colourless and light-coloured topaz.

Faceted blue topaz.

55

CLEAVAGE IN TOPAZ

Because topaz cleaves easily in a basal direction, rough topaz that has been weathered into soils or creeks is often found in the form of cleavage sections, rather than as whole crystals. These have two parallel faces (cleavage faces, not crystal faces) as well as a weathered or waterworn exterior. These cleavage sections can produce large, clear gemstones when faceted.

Blue topaz cleavage section with faceted stone.

FACETED TOPAZ

Topaz crystals often display a perfect termination, with one triangular face appearing to dominate the others. Interesting effects can be obtained in gem cutting by utilising as much as possible of the original crystal form. The stone pictured at top right was cut in an unusual design, which displays the optical perfection of the gem while echoing the shape of the former crystal. Topaz often occurs in large, inclusion-free crystals, making it a fine gem material; as in the picture below. Although lacking in fire, topaz is hard enough to take a strong polish, with an exceptionally brilliant result.

Faceted colourless topaz, above and below.

TOPAZ NOTES

Chemistry:	Aluminium fluorine silicate
Crystal system:	Orthorhombic
Hardness:	8
Refractive index:	1.610–1.638
Specific gravity:	3.53–3.56
Dispersion:	Low (0.014)
Cleavage:	Perfect
Lustre:	Vitreous

GARNET

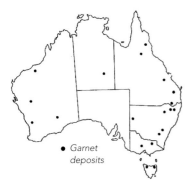

● *Garnet deposits*

Garnet is a general name for a group of minerals that share a similar chemical formula, a common crystal structure and similar physical properties. These complex silicates are almandine, pyrope, spessartine, grossular, andradite and uvarovite, of which only the first five are used as gemstones. Some garnets, like almandine and pyrope, form a gradually changing series from one to the other; others, like grossular and spessartine, do not.

Colour-zoned andradite in matrix.

Garnets are very common in metamorphic terrains in Australia. Almandine is found in rocks like schists, gneisses and amphibolite and also in pegmatites intruded into these rocks. In eastern Australia, pyrope-almandine is found in basaltic pipes, brought up from the lower crust or mantle. Grossular and andradite occur in contact-metamorphosed limestones called skarns. Spessartine comes from the manganese-rich, lead-zinc ore at Broken Hill.

PYROPE-ALMANDINE SERIES

The pyrope-almandine series of garnets supplies the type of red garnet widely known today and throughout history. Almandine is the iron-rich member while pyrope is magnesium-rich. An

Almandine crystal.

intermediate stage is known as rhodolite garnet.

These are found at a number of Australian localities and have, on occasion, been mistaken for rubies. If too dark for faceting they are cut as cabochons, giving them a rich, wine-red look.

SPESSARTINE

Spessartine is a manganese garnet, which has a colour range that runs from orange through to red. These garnets are usually faceted to make very bright gemstones. One particular characteristic that is found in spessartine garnets are feather-like, liquid inclusions.

Spessartine on matrix.

GROSSULAR

Grossular is a calcium garnet. It is often opaque but there are transparent gem varieties, one of which, hessonite, is found in Australia. Garnet crystals usually have a dodecahedral (12-sided) form.

Faceted grossular colour range.

Grossular crystal.

Faceted hessonites.

GROSSULAR COLOURS

Pure grossular is colourless but the addition of iron gives it a range of colours, from palest yellow though orange to deep red. Brownish yellow, orange and red colours, called hessonite, are found in the Harts Range, Northern Territory and provide a colourful alternative to the well-known red garnets of the pyrope-almandine series. Hessonite garnets are bright stones and some appear to intensify in colour under artificial light. Under magnification, they have a typically granular appearance, from numerous rounded, transparent inclusions of apatite or zircon. Another characteristic is 'treacly' streaks, which can give this stone a slightly 'oily' look.

GARNET NOTES

Chemistry:	Mostly aluminium silicates
Crystal system:	Cubic
Hardness:	6.5 – 7.5
Refractive index:	1.742–1.888
Specific gravity:	3.63–1.20
Dispersion:	Variable
Cleavage:	None
Lustre:	Vitreous to subadamantine

ZIRCON

• Zircon deposits

Zircon has been used as a gemstone throughout the ages. It has a broad colour range that varies from colourless through yellow, orange, brown, red, pink, violet, blue and green. These diverse colours are modified by minor amounts of elements such as hafnium, uranium, thorium and rare earths.

Zircon is an accessory mineral in many rocks and is occasionally found as large, gemmy crystals. Abundant sources of these are the alluvials from basaltic volcanic rocks in eastern Australia, which carried them up from hidden, lower crust and upper mantle sources. The Mud Tank carbonatite pipe in the Strangways Range in the Northern Territory, also provides a rich source.

Zircon crystal on matrix.

MUD TANK ZIRCONS

Zircons from the Strangways Range vary from colourless through pink shades to deep red, and through yellow shades to orange and brown. Although zircons are relatively hard, they are brittle and facet edges will abrade quickly with wear. When cut, zircons display almost as much fire as diamonds, and are usually cut as round brilliants.

IDENTIFYING ZIRCONS

Zircons are strongly doubly refractive and, under magnification, back facets appear doubled when viewed though the top of the stone. This is a simple identification aid, involving a 10 × lens. Before the widespread use of synthetics in jewellery, colourless zircons were used as a substitute for diamonds.

Mud Tank zircon colours.

Faceted zircons.

Faceted zircons, New England, NSW.

Zircon is commonly found with sapphire on the Australian sapphire fields and the Inverell area, New South Wales, produces some attractive cut stones. Zircons can change their colour with heat treatment. The colourless, blue and golden zircons that are widely used in jewellery are mostly heat-treated brown material. Sometimes these heat-induced colours fade on exposure to light but they may be restored with careful retreatment.

ZIRCON FLUORESCENCE

Pale-coloured zircons tend to have lower uranium contents than those of deeper colours. Uranium inhibits the fluorescence of zircon under ultraviolet light, so these low-uranium,

Low uranium zircons.

pale-coloured stones tend to fluoresce a strong yellow in this light.

STRUCTURAL CHANGE

Zircons that have a high uranium content have suffered a degree of structural breakdown over geological time, due to radiation. As a result of this radiation, their physical properties are slightly lower than for the other type and their structure is closer to amorphous. These zircons are known as metamict. In Australia, such stones tend to be dark red or brown.

Higher uranium zircons.

ZIRCON NOTES

Chemistry:	Zirconium silicate
Crystal system:	Tetragonal
Hardness:	7–7.5
Refractive index:	1.78–1.99
Specific gravity:	3.90–4.70
Dispersion:	High (0.039)
Cleavage:	Poor
Lustre:	Adamantine

SILICATE GEMSTONES

Silicates are the most common rock-forming minerals and are classified according to their chemistry and structure. They are compounds of, in decreasing order: oxygen, silicon, aluminium, iron, magnesium, calcium, sodium, potassium and other elements. Over 90 per cent of the Earth's crust is made up of silicate minerals, and most gemstones are silicates.

■ Jade
▲ Rhodonite
● Tourmaline

OLIVINE GROUP

Olivine is a name for mostly green magnesium, iron silicates that are plentiful in basalts and peridotite bodies. Transparent, green gemstones cut from this material are known as peridot. Olivine varies from a preponderance of magnesium at one end of a mineral series to iron at the other. Too much iron imparts a brownish appearance and the most attractive peridots are those with prominent magnesium.

Olivine in matrix.

PERIDOT

Peridot has a distinctive yellow-green colour and an 'oily' lustre. Its hardness is 6.5, slightly less than quartz. Because of its high birefringence (double refraction), doubling of the back facets can be observed with magnification; (SG 3.34).

FELDSPAR GROUP

Feldspars are some of the most common rock-forming minerals. Their name means 'field stone', expressing their abundance. Feldspars are aluminium silicates with either potassium, sodium or calcium. They form in two chemically distinct groups: alkali feldspars (sodium, potassium) and plagioclase feldspars (sodium, calcium). Alkali feldspars contain yellow orthoclase, 'moonstone' and 'amazonite'; plagioclase includes andesine, labradorite and 'sunstone'.

Faceted peridot.

Yellow andesine crystal.

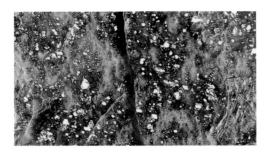

'Sunstone' feldspar (magnified).

PLAGIOCLASE FELDSPARS

Plagioclase feldspars are usually opaque greyish minerals, sometimes with a bright blue spectral sheen (called labradorescence). In Australia, however, the variety andesine occurs in a transparent, light yellow form that yields large, clear, attractive gems. Hardness is around 6–6.5 and cleavage is perfect in two directions, so care is needed when cutting or handling these gemstones (SG about 2.68).

Faceted andesine feldspar.

'SUNSTONE' AND 'MOONSTONE'

A variety of plagioclase feldspar found in Australia is known as 'sunstone' due to its spangled, golden-bronze appearance. The spangled effect, termed 'aventurescence' comes from a myriad of minute, hematite inclusions that reflect light. Hardness is 6–6.5; SG is 2.62–2.65.

Anorthoclase, a colourless, transparent variety with a bluish sheen, is called 'moonstone'.

TOURMALINE GROUP

Tourmaline covers several complex borosilicates with variable chemical compositions. Slightly harder than quartz (7.0–7.5), it also lacks cleavage and is very stable (SG 3.00– 3.12). Tourmaline has the greatest colour range of any gemstone. In Australia, it is commonly opaque and black (schorl). Fine gem tourmaline has been mined at Kangaroo Island, South Australia, where the largest crystal found cut a deep blue stone of over 14 carats, and the Coolgardie area, Western Australia, which produces mainly blue and green material.

Faceted tourmaline.

NEPHRITE JADE

Jade is an umbrella term covering two mainly green silicates, jadeite and nephrite, that have been used throughout human history for jewellery, carved objects and weapons. As well as colour, they share a tough microcrystalline structure. Jadeite does not occur in Australia but there are two significant deposits of nephrite jade: one at Cowell in South Australia and the other near Tamworth in New South Wales.

Swan carved from SA nephrite jade.

at Cowell in South Australia is medium- to fine-grained and mostly deep green to black, although as many as 18 colours have been catalogued.

NEW SOUTH WALES NEPHRITE

Nephrite is translucent to opaque and, because of its toughness, takes a very high polish. It is an excellent carving material and is suitable for cabochons and beads. Nephrite from the Tamworth area is generally lighter in colour than Cowell jade. Light and medium greens

Nephrite jade (magnified).

Nephrite is a magnesium, iron, calcium silicate and is a variety of the tremolite–ferro-actinolite mineral series. Nephrite jade is usually rich in magnesium (tremolite) in attractive shades of green, yellow or cream (descriptively called 'mutton fat'). A high iron content darkens the colour to deep green or black (actinolite–ferro-actinolite). The SG varies accordingly, from 2.90 to 3.10.

SOUTH AUSTRALIAN NEPHRITE

Although the hardness of nephrite is less than quartz (6.0–6.5), comparative tests have proved it to be the toughest natural mineral known. Its toughness is the result of a structure of interlocking fibrous crystals, often described as 'felted'. Nephrite from the large deposits

Pendant carved from NSW nephrite jade.

predominate, while amber shades and unusual flowing and flecked patterns are sometimes found.

RHODONITE

Rhodonite is a manganese, calcium silicate. It belongs to the triclinic crystal system and occurs in both crystallised and massive form (SG 3.40–3.70). Fine, red, transparent crystals on matrix are found at Broken Hill in New South Wales. While it is preferable that such fine mineral specimens not be mutilated, excellent gemstones for collectors are, on rare occasions, faceted from loose or broken crystals of such material.

Polished rhodonite slice.

appearance. Deposits occur at Danglemah in New South Wales.

CHRYSOCOLLA

Chrysocolla is a hydrated copper silicate with a rich, blue-green colour. It is often intergrown with other copper minerals, like turquoise and malachite. It is micro-crystalline and semi-translucent to opaque. Chrysocolla is a fairly soft mineral with a hardness range of 2–4, or even as high as 6 if quartz is present. It can be cut and polished into attractive cabochons, which need careful handling.

Faceted rhodonite, Broken Hill.

POLISHED RHODONITE

Rhodonite occurs more commonly in a massive aggregate form and is polished as an ornamental gem material (H 6). It is pale pink to almost red in colour and streaked with black manganese oxide. It has a characteristic 'sugary'

Chrysocolla veins in matrix (magnified).

PREHNITE

Prehnite is a hydrated calcium, aluminium silicate. It can be coloured light green, yellow, golden brown or orange and generally forms grape-like aggregates of radiating fibrous crystals in some basic igneous rocks. It is translucent to opaque with a hardness of 6.0–6.5 and an SG of 2.88–2.94. Fine, large mineral specimens, as well as gemstones, have come from Prospect in New South Wales.

Faceted prehnite.

Attractive yellow-green prehnite comes from Wave Hill in the Northern Territory.

CORDIERITE (IOLITE)

Cordierite is a magnesium, iron, aluminium silicate, with a colour range that includes light to dark blue, violet, grey, yellow, brown and colourless. Blue is the preferred colour for gemstones. Gem quality cordierite is called 'iolite' by gemmologists. In the past, it has been misleadingly termed 'water sapphire' because of a resemblance to corundum. It can be translucent to transparent and has a hardness of 7–7.5 and an SG of 2.57–2.66.

Prehnite in matrix.

POLISHED PREHNITE

Prehnite is an unusual gemstone, with a waxy to subvitreous lustre. Although it is often flawed, prehnite at its best quality makes an attractive ornamental material. It is found in large sizes and is generally cut into cabochons or may be carved. When translucent, prehnite can be faceted into interesting freeform shapes.

Cordierite crystal.

65

FACETED IOLITE

Cordierite (iolite) crystallises in the orthorhombic system and has one outstanding physical property, which is its strong pleochroism. It shows light blue, dark blue and yellow from different light directions, an effect that can be observed with the unaided eye. Attractive, large gemstones have been faceted from material from the Entia Valley, Harts Range, Northern Territory.

Kyanite crystals.

TITANITE (SPHENE)

Titanite, called 'sphene' by gemmologists, is a titanium, calcium silicate with a colour range of yellow, brown and green. Several properties make it an unusual gemstone. Very high dispersion makes it particularly fiery. It has a very high birefringence (double refraction) and the doubling of facets, seen through the table of the stone, gives it a slightly blurry look. It is also observably pleochroic, showing three colours (yellow, red and green) in one stone. Titanite is rather soft, with a hardness of 5.5 and its specific gravity is 3.52–3.54. Fine stones come from the Northern Territory.

Faceted iolite.

KYANITE

Kyanite is an aluminium silicate, with the same chemical formula as andalusite and sillimanite but a different crystal system. It is colourless to blue or blue-green, often colour-zoned and occasionally chatoyant. A unique feature is its variable hardness, which is 7 across the crystal width and 5 along the crystal length. Kyanite has strong pleochroism (colourless, light blue, dark blue) and perfect cleavage. Specific gravity is 3.65–3.69. It is a collector's stone, since a transparent gem-quality stone is rare and the cleavage makes it challenging to cut.

Faceted sphene.

OTHER GEMSTONES

Australia produces small quantities of other gem minerals which, at their best, are used as ornamentals and gemstones. Turquoise, malachite, variscite, apatite and fluorite, to mention some, are sought after by fossickers and lapidary groups, and sometimes appear as by-products of commercial mining operations.

• Turquoise
▲ Malachite   ▪ Fluorite
✦ Variscite   ✱ Apatite

TURQUOISE GROUP

Throughout history turquoise has been prized for its bright blue colour, although it can also be blue-green and green. It is opaque and often mottled and veined by dark matrix—a feature considered attractive. Turquoise is a hydrous copper, aluminium phosphate containing some iron. Crystals are very rare and it is generally found in massive form. Turquoise takes a good polish (H 5–6) and it has an SG of 2.60–2.85.

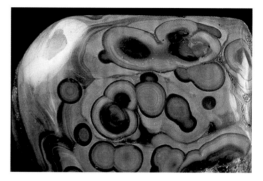
Polished malachite.

Turquoise seam.

MALACHITE

Malachite has a distinctive dark and light green, concentrically banded appearance. It is opaque and is widely used as an ornamental material. Malachite is a hydrated copper carbonate, which forms monoclinic crystals but is usually found in

grape-like mounds of fibrous, radiating crystals. It is fairly soft (H 3.5–4) and the SG is 3.74–3.95.

VARISCITE

Variscite is green to greenish blue in colour and can be translucent to opaque. It is used as an ornamental material and made into carvings, cabochons or beads. Variscite is a

Variscite in matrix.

hydrous aluminium phosphate containing some chromium and iron. It is moderately soft (H 3.5–5) and has a waxy to vitreous lustre. Large sizes are available and its SG is 2.40–2.60.

APATITE GROUP

Apatite ranges from colourless to yellow,

Apatite: faceted stone with crystal.

brown, pink, blue, green, violet and purple. It is transparent to translucent and occasionally chatoyant. Apatite is a calcium phosphate, which also contains fluorine or chlorine. Most gem specimens are fluorine-rich, with a hardness of 5 and an SG of 3.17–3.23. A yellow-green apatite from the Strangways Range in the Northern Territory, is sometimes faceted.

FLUORITE

Once known as fluorspar, fluorite has a wide range of colours and is often colour-zoned. It is used as an ornamental and sometimes faceted. Most varieties fluoresce strongly under ultraviolet light. Fluorite is a calcium fluoride that crystallises in the cubic system. Its perfect octahedral cleavage makes it a difficult stone to cut. The hardness is 4 and the SG is around 3.18. Australia produces attractive fluorites from Emmaville in New South Wales, and Luina in Tasmania.

Faceted pink fluorite (437 ct).

Faceted green fluorite (147 ct).

CASSITERITE

Cassiterite can be colourless to yellow, brown and deep, wine red. When transparent to translucent, material is sometimes cut as a gemstone for collectors. Cassiterite is tin oxide (H 6–7 and SG 6.80–7.00). The very high dispersion and lustre makes it a very fiery, faceted gemstone.

Polished cassiterite.

PEARLS

One of Australia's most valuable and important gems is not a mineral but an organic material. Pearls grow in the bodies of molluscs (shellfish) as a response to intrusion by a parasite. To protect its soft body, the mollusc secretes calcium carbonate, forming a concretion that consists of a small, central nucleus surrounded by concentric layers of the same mother-of-pearl (nacre) from which it builds its shell. Natural pearls are rare and most pearls are now cultivated or cultured. A bead or section of tissue is inserted into a suitable mollusc to form the nucleus of a cultured pearl.

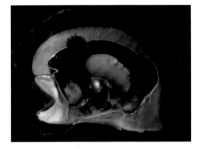
Cultured pearl in oyster.

• Pearls

The beauty of pearls lies in their shimmering iridescent lustre. In the waters off the north-western coast of Australia, South Sea pearls are harvested from the large oyster Pinctada maxima. The largest known is a perfect, round pearl of 20.8 mm.

EARL COLOURS
Colours vary from silver-white through shades of cream, light and deep gold, peach and pink. Sometimes an unusual bronze, blue or green colour appears. Perfect white pearls are the most sought after and expensive specimens.

PEARL SHAPES
Australian South Sea pearls are generally over 10 mm in size and come in a variety of shapes. Symmetrical shapes are more sought-after and the most valuable are perfect, round pearls with an unblemished surface and a high lustre.

Australian South Sea pearl colours.

69

BAROQUE PEARLS

Oysters grow pearls in many shapes. Pearls with an irregular and asymmetrical shape are called 'baroque'. These baroque pearls are popular in jewellery and sometimes an unusually shaped baroque pearl will have a piece individually designed for it.

Baroque pearls.

MABE PEARLS

Mabe pearls are not grown in the body of the oyster but against the inside shell. They are cultured blister pearls—half spheres with flat or rounded bases. A bead is fixed to the inside shell and the resulting blister pearl is removed and given a new base. Such pearls are used for earrings, brooches and rings.

Mabe pearls.

KESHI PEARLS

Keshi pearls are non-nucleated pearls that sometimes form spontaneously in oysters that have been returned to the water after the harvesting of a crop of cultured pearls. They are attractive, lustrous and come in different shapes, colours and sizes.

Keshi pearls.

MATCHING PEARLS

Because perfect, round pearls are rare, a necklace of such pearls in matching, or perfectly graduated, sizes takes much skill and time to assemble. Many tens of thousands of pearls must be sorted to do so.

Matched and graduated pearls.

ORNAMENTAL GALLERY

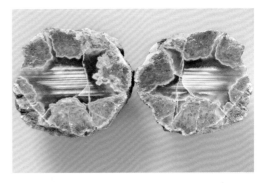

Thunder egg with agate, Boggabri, NSW.

Agate slice, polished, Agate Creek, Qld.

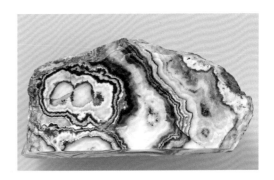

Polished agate, Drake, NSW.

71

Ornamental Gallery

Polished agate, Katherine, NT.

Blue lace agate, Monto, Qld.

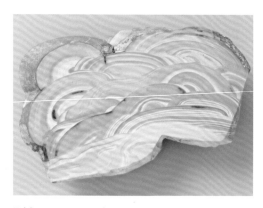

'Ribbonstone', Mooka Station, WA.

GOLD AND PLATINUM MINERALS

Gold is one of the noble metals and is the foremost gold mineral. Australia's goldfields are world famous, particularly the historic Victorian and Kalgoorlie 'Golden Mile', Western Australian fields. There are numerous gold producers in Australia and ore deposits are still being found. Gold can mix with other elements, particularly silver and mercury, to form alloys such as electrum and amalgam. Gold also combines with tellurium to form gold telluride minerals. These are rare, but are well-developed around Kalgoorlie.

• *Gold deposits*

GOLD

The yellow-gold colour and streak and metallic lustre, combined with its soft (H 2.5–3) and very dense (SG 15.6–19.3) nature are characteristic. Crystals (cubic) are easily damaged due to their malleable nature. Novices may confuse flecks of other yellowish minerals with gold, the so-called 'fool's gold' minerals—pyrite, chalcopyrite and altered mica.

GOLD CRYSTALS

Gold forms crystals, but well-formed crystals are uncommon. Octahedral shapes are typical, but there are also rounded, wiry, branching, leafy, mesh-like or even skeleton shapes. Flattened scales and grains are common, sometimes occurring in thin sheets.

Crystallised gold on matrix.

Octahedral gold crystals.

73

GOLD NUGGETS

Because of its density, released gold often concentrates near its source (eluvial gold) or will wash further away (alluvial gold). Some gold is deposited from groundwaters in soil horizons to form irregularly shaped nuggets. Australia is famous for large nuggets, which are still being found.

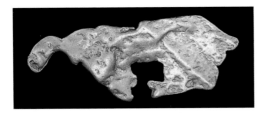

Gold nugget.

CALAVERITE

This rare gold, tellurium mineral appears in the classic Kalgoorlie ore. It is silver–white in colour, often with a yellowish tinge. Small lath-like crystals (monoclinic) occur, but granular to crystalline masses are typical. It is soft (H 2.5) and dense (SG 9).

Calaverite in matrix.

KRENNERITE

Krennerite and sylvanite are rare gold and silver, tellurium minerals, and both appear in Kalgoorlie gold ores. Krennerite is silver-white to brassy yellow in colour. Crystals often form prisms (orthorhombic) with a perfect cleavage. They are soft (H 2.5) and heavy (SG over 8).

Krennerite in matrix.

PLATINUM MINERALS

These often associate with silica-poor rocks, but are rare. Platinum forms grains, scaly crystals (cubic) and nuggets. Its steel grey, metallic colour, moderate hardness (H 4–4.5) and high density (SG 14–19) are distinctive.

Platinum nugget.

SILVER MINERALS

Silver is rarer than gold but it enters into more minerals than gold. It mixes with gold, copper and other metals in limited amounts to form alloys. Silver frequents weathered silver or lead-zinc ore deposits. Unlike gold, silver alters when released, so it does not survive in alluvial deposits. Important silver deposits in Australia include ore bodies in the Broken Hill region, around New England and at Elura mine, Cobar, in New South Wales, and at Teutonic Bore in Western Australia. A large mass of silver (2000 ounces) was mined at Elizabeth Hill, Pilbara, Western Australia in 2000. Silver has an affinity for antimony and arsenic and the halide elements—chlorine, bromine and iodine. The Broken Hill weathered alteration zone is a classic world locality for silver halides.

Silver in matrix.

Although its silver-white colour tarnishes grey to black, the streak is silver-white. Crystals (cubic) are often distorted and form needles, mesh-works, branches or fibres. It has metallic to dull lustre and is soft (H 2.5–3) and heavy (SG 10.1–11.1).

DYSCRASITE

This silver, antimony mineral formed exceptional crystals at Broken Hill in NSW. Crystals (orthorhombic) are silver-white in colour and streak. They have a metallic lustre and sometimes tarnish yellow to black. It is soft (H 3.5–4) and heavy (SG 9.4–10.0).

STEPHANITE

Stephanite, a brittle silver ore, is a silver, antimony and sulfur mineral. It is iron-black in colour, metallic and opaque, and crystals (orthorhombic) are soft (H 2–2.5) and dense (SG 6.2–6.5).

Dyscrasite on matrix.

75

Stephanite crystal mass.

Proustite on matrix.

CHLORARGYRITE

This silver and chlorine mineral can contain some bromine and is known as 'horn silver' because of its shape. It is often found at Broken Hill. It is grey-green to yellow, grading to grey. Crystals (cubic) are rare and the mineral is usually massive, resembling wax or horn. It is very soft (H 1–1.5) and reasonably dense (SG 5.5).

Chlorargyrite, bromine-rich.

PROUSTITE

Proustite is a silver, arsenic and sulfur mineral and, with pyragyrite, is one of the 'ruby silver' ores. It is scarlet to vermilion in colour and

streak. The bright lustre blackens on prolonged exposure to light. Crystals (trigonal) are twinned and show distinct cleavage but also form in compact masses. It is soft (H 2–2.5) and heavy (SG 5.5–5.7).

IODARYGYRITE

This rare silver and iodine mineral appears at Broken Hill. Nearly colourless, it becomes pale yellow to green on exposure to light. Crystals (hexagonal) usually form thin plates and show perfect cleavage. It is soft (H 1.5) and heavy (SG 7).

Iodargyrite crystal mass.

COPPER MINERALS: COMMON ALTERATIONS

Copper minerals are widespread in Australian ore deposits and some form important economic sources of the metal. They are found both in primary ores and secondary alteration zones. Copper is found in some alteration zones, as in Broken

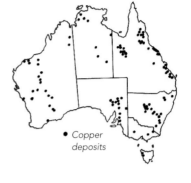

Hill and in other New South Wales and north Queensland deposits. The most abundant copper alteration minerals are copper carbonate minerals, such as azurite and malachite. The

• Copper deposits

blue of azurite and green of malachite are often used as prospecting pointers for copper deposits. Copper silicate, chrysocolla, is another common copper alteration mineral.

Copper with gypsum.

COPPER

The copper-red colour, shining metallic copper streak, softness (H 2.5–3) and dense nature (SG 8.8–8.9) are characteristic. Copper crystallises in different combinations of the cubic system. However, it is often branched, wiry, filament-like or twisted in form. Bizarre skeleton-like forms and twinned crystals can develop. Dusty or velvety veneers of green copper alteration minerals can coat crystals.

Copper crystals.

AZURITE

This copper, carbon, oxygen, hydrogen mineral is typically azure to dark blue in colour, with a paler blue streak. Crystals (monoclinic) vary in shape but are often wedge-shaped and show cleavage. They are highly translucent and have a bright lustre. Azurite can be massive to earthy in form. The mineral is fairly soft (H 3.5–4) and moderately dense (SG 3.7–3.9).

Azurite crystals.

MALACHITE

Another copper, carbon, oxygen and hydrogen mineral, malachite is more prevalent than azurite. It is typically bright green with a pale green streak. Crystals (monoclinic) are rarely distinct and form needles, tufts and rosettes. Bunched grape-like and stalactitic forms are often present. Translucent to opaque, it is silky to very bright in lustre. It is fairly soft (H 3.5–4), with a moderate density (SG 3.9–4.1).

Malachite on matrix.

MALACHITE AND AZURITE

These two copper, hydroxy carbonate minerals often appear together, sometimes with the malachite replacing what was formerly azurite.

Malachite and azurite.

Malachite contains a higher percentage of copper than azurite. Their specific colours and azurite's better crystal shape make them easy to distinguish.

CHRYSOCOLLA

This copper, silicon, oxygen and hydrogen mineral sometimes replaces other copper minerals, such as azurite. It typically ranges from green into light blue and has a white streak. Crystals are invisible and the texture is generally smooth to earthy. Crust, seams or grape-like forms occur. It is translucent to opaque with a glassy lustre, soft (H 2–4) and low in density (SG 2–2.3).

Chrysocolla replacment of azurite crystals.

COPPER MINERALS: MAIN ORES

Many copper-producing mines dot the Australian landscape; some are associated with gold or other metal deposits. Major deposits include Mt Lyell in Tasmania; North Parkes, Cadia and Cobar, in New South Wales; Mt Isa–Cloncurry and Mt Morgan–Rockhampton, in Queensland; early historic fields, Olympic Dam and Mt Gunson in South Australia; Golden Grove and Nifty in Western Australia and Tennant Creek in the Northern Territory. The most important primary copper ore minerals are copper sulfides and copper oxides. Some of these concentrate in enrichment zones above the main primary ores. A host of other copper minerals contain antimony, arsenic and bismuth, and also appear in many ores.

CUPRITE

Known as red copper ore, cuprite is a copper and oxygen mineral. It takes different shades of red, with a brownish red streak. Crystals (cubic) show cleavage and are sometimes elongated into needles. Lustre varies from dull metallic to very bright. The mineral shows a curved fracture, it is fairly soft (H 3.5–4) and dense (SG 5.8–6.2).

Cuprite crystals, malachite-coated.

BORNITE

Often called peacock ore, bornite is a copper, iron, sulfur mineral. Copper-red to brown when it has fresh surfaces, it takes on an iridescent tarnish when exposed to air. The streak is

Iridescent bornite.

greyish black. Crystals (cubic) are rare. Often massive, opaque and metallic in lustre, it is soft (H 3) with moderate density (SG 4.1–4.3).

CHALCOPYRITE

Called copper pyrites, the mineral contains copper, iron and sulfur. It is brassy yellow, with a greenish black streak but often tarnishes or becomes iridescent. Crystals are common (tetragonal) and show cleavage but the mineral is often massive. It is opaque, metallic, brittle and shows uneven fracture. A fairly soft mineral (H 3.5–4), it is moderately dense (SG 4.1–4.3).

Chalcopyrite crystals.

Chalcocite crystal.

COVELLITE

A copper and sulfur mineral, covellite is dark blue and has a lead-grey to black streak. Crystals (hexagonal) are normally thin hexagonal plates with strong cleavage, but the massive form is common. Covellite is opaque with metallic lustre, fairly soft (H 3.5–4) and moderately heavy (SG 4.1–4.3).

Covellite in matrix.

CHALCOCITE

Called copper glance, chalcocite is a copper and sulfur mineral. Colour and streak are blackish lead-grey but it can tarnish blue or green. Crystals (orthorhombic) show indistinct cleavage, curved fracture and are sometimes twinned. Massive form is common and the lustre is metallic. It is soft (H 2.5–3) and dense (SG 5.5–5.8).

TETRAHEDRITE

Termed grey copper ore, this sums up the colour and streak of the mineral. It is a copper, antimony and sulfur mineral, but can tuck up to 30 per cent silver into its structure. Crystals (cubic) are usually tetrahedral pyramids, or else it is massive. It is fairly soft (H 3–4) and moderately dense (SG 4.4–5.1).

Tetrahedrite crystals.

COPPER MINERALS: RARITIES

Copper enters many minerals. Among the rarer types are halogen-element compounds (chlorides, bromides, iodides) and various arsenates, phosphates and sulfates. A copper chloride mineral is atacamite found in early copper mining in South Australia. A copper iodide from Broken Hill was the first new mineral recorded from there, and was named marshite after CW Marsh, who described it. Rare copper-arsenate minerals, clinoclase and conichalcite, come from Dome Rock, Olary in South Australia. An intriguing copper phosphate is pseudomalachite, found at Tottenham in New South Wales. As it resembles malachite, it is easily misidentified and may be more common than supposed. A colourful sulfate found at Broken Hill is linarite, which matches the blue of azurite.

Linarite on matrix.

ATACAMITE

This copper, chlorine, oxygen and hydrogen mineral appears in alteration ore zones. Bright to dark green, it has a green streak and forms slender, striated crystals (orthorhombic) with

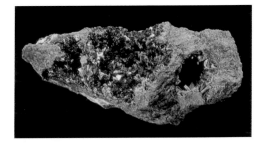

Atacamite in matrix.

excellent cleavage. Very bright to glassy in lustre, it shows a curved fracture. Fairly soft (H 3–3.5) and moderately dense (SG 3.7–3.8).

LINARITE

A coupling of copper and lead combining with sulfur, oxygen and hydrogen, linarite is a rare alteration mineral known from Broken Hill. Deep blue crystals (monoclinic) show distinct cleavages and are soft (H 2.5) and fairly dense (SG 5.4).

MARSHITE

This copper and iodine mineral is very rare but it does occur at Broken Hill. Pink to deep red, it deepens in colour when it is exposed to air. Crystals (cubic) are often tetrahedral pyramids with striated faces and it shows a good cleavage. It is transparent with waxy lustre, soft (H 2–3) and dense (SG 5.6).

Marshite on matrix.

CLINOCLASE

This mineral combines copper, arsenic, oxygen and hydrogen. It is dark green to blue-green with a bluish green streak. Crystals (monoclinic) form prisms, sometimes being elongated. These often group in spherical forms with radiating fibres. Usually translucent, with glassy to resinous lustre, the mineral is soft (H 2.5–3) and moderately dense (SG 4.2–4.4).

Clinoclase in matrix.

CONICHALCITE

A similar copper, arsenic, oxygen and hydrogen mineral to clinoclase, conichalcite has more calcium and water in its structure. Yellow to emerald-green crystals (orthorhombic)

Conichalcite on matrix.

are usually fibrous. It resembles malachite, which is the common copper hydroxy carbonate mineral. It is harder (at 4.5) than clinoclase, but similar in density (SG 4.1).

PSEUDOMALACHITE

This mineral combines copper with phosphorus, oxygen and hydrogen. The green colour and streak closely resembles that of malachite. Crystals (monoclinic) rarely develop and it is usually fibrous and massive in form. It is moderately hard (at 4.5) being slightly harder than malachite, and it is moderately dense (SG 3.6).

Grape-like pseudomalachite.

LEAD MINERALS: MAIN ORES

Lead minerals are well represented in both large as well as many small ore deposits. They commonly accompany zinc and silver mineralisation. Some deposits mark ancient sea-floor hot spring accumulations while others represent warm mineral solution replacements of former limestones. Important lead, zinc deposits include Broken Hill and Woodlawn in New South Wales; Mt Isa in Queensland; Read–Rosebery and Helleyer–Que River mines in Tasmania; Woodcutters mine, Pine Creek in the Northern Territory and Lennard Shelf mines in Western Australia.

Galena is the main, primary lead-ore mineral, but galena also forms in secondary alteration zones. Typical secondary lead minerals are cerussite, a lead carbonate, and anglesite, a lead sulfate. Rare lead carbonates also occur, for example dundasite in western Tasmania.

• Lead deposits

Primary galena ore.

GALENA
Called 'lead glance', galena is a lead and sulfur mineral. Colour and streak are lead-grey. It is opaque with metallic lustre. Crystals (cubic) are typically cubes or combinations of cubes with octahedral faces, with perfect cubic cleavage. Twinning may be present. It is soft (H 2.5–2.8) and quite dense (SG 7.4–7.6).

CERUSSITE
A lead, carbon and oxygen mineral, cerussite is called white lead ore and grades from white into grey, with a colourless streak. Crystals (orthorhombic) are often tabular or pyramidal

Secondary galena.

Cerussite twin.

and twinned. Elongate crystals form spectacular mesh-works. They show transparency and the lustre can range from resinous, pearly, glassy to very bright. It is fairly soft (H 3–3.5) and dense (SG 6.4–6.6).

ANGLESITE

In its white colour form, this lead, sulfur and oxygen mineral often resembles cerussite. However, unlike cerussite, its colours can extend to yellow and green tinges. Crystals (orthorhombic) are often prismatic, tabular or pyramidal and twinning is uncommon. It shows distinct cleavage and is very brittle with a curved fracture. Angesite is marginally softer (H 2.7–3) than cerussite, but similar in density (SG 6.3–6.4).

Anglesite crystals

'CHROME'CERUSSITE

This rare, yellow cerussite comes from a few western Tasmanian mines. It accompanies crocoite, the bright orange-red lead chromate, and the two colourful minerals together prove very attractive. The yellow colour has been assigned to chromium impurity, but analyses show negligible amounts, leaving the cause of its colour a mystery and the name a misnomer.

'Chrome' cerussite crystals.

DUNDASITE

This rare lead, carbon, oxygen, hydrogen mineral was named in 1893 from Dundas in western Tasmania. Creamy to snowy white, it forms small spheroidal aggregates of radiating needles (orthorhombic). The surface adopts greenish to bluish colours, giving it visual appeal. Near-transparent crystals show strong cleavage and silky to glassy lustre. It is soft (H 2) with lowish density (SG 3.2–3.3).

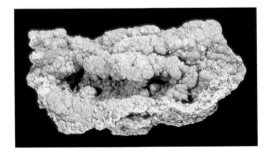

Spheroidal dundasite.

LEAD MINERALS: COMMON ALTERATIONS

Some lead minerals in alteration zones incorporate elements such as phosphorus, arsenic and chlorine. The pyromorphite–mimetite series is prominent, going from lead, chlorine, phosphorus-rich members to lead, chlorine, arsenic-rich members. Rarer minerals of such elements are also found in some western Tasmanian mines.

PYROMORPHITE

Pyromorphite is commonly green, but it ranges in colour through white, grey, yellow, brown, orange, with a white to pale yellow streak. Crystals (hexagonal) are often prismatic, sometimes barrel-shaped or branching. Crystals show some transparency and resinous lustre. Globular, wart-, grape- or kidney-like forms occur. The mineral is moderately soft (H 3.5–4) and dense (SG 6.5–7.1).

Pyromorphite crystals.

MIMETITE

The mineral mimetite has a resemblance to pyromorphite, (hexagonal) but it is usually yellow, yellow-orange or brown and the streak is white. It has similar hardness (3.5) and density (SG 7.0–7.3).

Mimetite on matrix.

PHOSGENITE

This lead, chlorine, carbon and oxygen mineral is white to grey or yellow, with a white streak. Crystals (tetragonal) are usually prismatic, sometimes tabular and show distinct cleavage. The mineral is transparent to translucent, very bright in lustre, soft (H 2.7–3), and dense (SG 6.0–6.3).

Phosgenite on matrix.

85

● *Molybdenum deposits*

MOLYBDENUM MINERALS

Minerals of the heavy metal element molybdenum have some economic importance. The main ore mineral is molybdenite, and a prominent secondary mineral is wulfenite. Molybdenum commonly associates with tungsten in deposits, as at Kingsgate–Tenterfield and the inland south coast in New South Wales; Mt Arthur, the Cairns hinterland and Townsville–Charters Towers areas in Queensland; Moly Hill in the Northern Territory and Mt Mulgine in Western Australia.

MOLYBDENITE

Molybdenite is a molybdenum sulfide. Pure lead-grey in colour, it has a greenish grey streak. Crystals are mostly hexagonal shapes and may also be tabular or prismatic. They can form rose-like groups. Strong cleavage imparts a sheeted or scaly form. Sheets are flexible. The mineral has bright metallic lustre, is very soft (H 1–1.5), and moderately dense (SG 4.7–4.8).

WULFENITE

This lead, molybdenum and oxygen mineral ranges in colour through white, grey, yellow, orange, green, brown and red but it has a white streak. Crystals (tetragonal) often form tablets or thin wafers, with cleavage, and show translucency with resinous to very bright lustre. Twinning is common and granular to massive forms occur. It is soft (H 2.7–3) and dense (SG 6.7–7.0).

Molybdenite crystal rose.

Wulfenite on matrix.

ZINC AND CADMIUM MINERALS

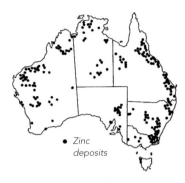

Zinc deposits

Zinc minerals accompany lead and copper ores and dominate some deposits. Large zinc reserves include Mt Isa, Queensland; Broken Hill-Cobar and Woodlawn, New South Wales; Read-Rosebery and Helleyer–Que River mines, Tasmania; Woodcutters mine, Pine Creek, Northern Territory, and Lennard Shelf and Sorby deposits, Western Australia. Dominant zinc deposits include Elura mine, Cobar, New South Wales; Thalanga–Charters Towers, Lawn Hill and Century mine, Queensland; HYC Mines, McArthur Basin, Northern Territory; Puttapa mine, Beltana, South Australia. Cadmium is sometimes allied with zinc, but only rarely is it concentrated enough to form a separate mineral.

SPHALERITE

Sphalerite is a zinc and sulfur mineral; often darkened by incorporation of some iron. It is pale to yellow, reddish brown or black, with a white, light yellow or brownish streak. Crystals (cubic) are often tetrahedral in shape, commonly twinned and show perfect cleavage. Lustre varies from resinous to very bright. With a curved fracture, sphalerite is moderate in hardness (3.5–4).

CHALCOPHANITE

This zinc, iron, manganese, oxygen and hydrogen mineral forms alteration caps in zinc deposits. Bluish to iron-black, it has a chocolate-brown streak. Crystals (trigonal) are small, with perfect cleavage, and these form glistening coatings. Grape-like and stalactitic forms of the mineral are common. Chalcophanite is particularly soft (H 2.5) and moderately dense (SG 4.0).

Sphalerite in massive form.

Chalcophanite in matrix.

SMITHSONITE

This zinc, carbon and oxygen mineral ranges from white through grey, green, brown and blue. Crystals (trigonal) are rare and grape-like; stalactitic and encrusting forms are common. Some transparency shows and lustre ranges from glassy to near pearly. It is moderately hard (H 5.5) and moderately dense (SG 4.3–4.5).

Smithsonite in globular form.

TARBUTTITE

Tarbuttite is a rare zinc, phosphorus, oxygen and hydrogen mineral from Reephook Hill, South Australia. Colourless to white crystals (triclinic) are usually stout to prismatic. Sheaf-like masses are found. Lustre is vitreous to pearly. The mineral is moderately hard (3.5–4) and moderately dense (SG 4.1).

Tarbuttite crystals, partly coated.

SCHOLZITE

Relatively rare, scholzite is a calcium, zinc, phosphorus, oxygen and hydrogen mineral from Reephook Hill in South Australia. It was also found recently at Broken Hill. Colourless to white, it has a vitreous lustre. Crystals (orthorhombic) are often well-developed and elongate. It is moderately hard (H 4) with fairly low density (SG 3.1).

Scholzite in matrix.

GREENOCKITE

This cadmium and sulfur mineral ranges from yellow, orange or red both in colour and streak. Crystals (hexagonal) favour pyramidal shapes and show cleavage. Lustre ranges from glassy to resinous, but may be dull in thin coatings. It is softish (H 3–3.5) and moderately dense (SG 4.8–4.9).

Greenockite on matrix.

ANTIMONY, BISMUTH AND TANTALUM MINERALS

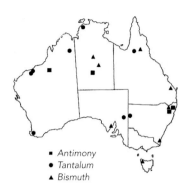

A NTIMONY minerals are particularly allied to gold-bearing quartz veins in eastern Australia. Uncombined antimony is rare, and the main ore is stibnite. Alteration minerals occur, such as kermesite.

BISMUTH minerals include bismuth and bismuth sulfides. Main localities include New England, Temora and Pambula areas, New South Wales; Cairns hinterland and Biggenden, Queensland; Balhanna, South Australia; and Tennant Creek, Northern Territory.

TANTALUM, a heavy metal element, associates with elements like niobium (alias columbium), tin and tungsten. Tantalum and niobium minerals come from granite pegmatite regions, particularly in Western Australia.

STIBNITE

This antimony and sulfur mineral can carry gold and silver. Both the colour and the streak are lead- to steel-grey. Crystals (orthorhombic) are commonly bladed, often curved, twisted or bent, or in radiating needles; they are striated and show perfect cleavage. The mineral is opaque, with metallic to very bright lustre, soft (H 2) and moderately dense (SG 4.5–4.6).

Stibnite crystals.

KERMESITE

An antimony, sulfur and oxygen mineral, kermesite results from the alteration of stibnite. It is cherry-red with a red-brown streak. Crystals (triclinic) are platy or needle-like. Lustre can be very bright and the mineral is very soft (H 1–1.5) and moderately dense (SG 4.7).

Kermesite on matrix.

BISMUTH

Colour and streak are both silver-white, but they tarnish. Crystals (trigonal) usually form mesh-like, branching or granular masses. Opaque, with metallic lustre, the mineral is soft (H 2.5) and noticeably dense (SG 9.8).

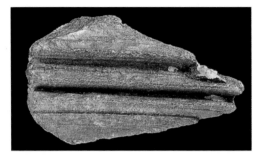

Bismuth crystals.

BISMUTHINITE

This bismuth and sulfur mineral is lead-grey in colour and streak. Crystals (orthorhombic) are elongated with perfect cleavage. Massive, sheet-like or fibrous forms occur. The mineral is opaque, with metallic lustre, soft (H 2), and dense (SG 6.4–6.5).

Bismuthinite crystals.

TANTALITE-(Mn)

This manganese, iron, tantalum, niobium and oxygen mineral is black, brownish black or orange-red, with dark red to black streak. Crystals (orthorhombic) are mostly prismatic to tabular, show distinct cleavage and are often twinned. It is opaque, with subdued metallic lustre, hard (H 6–6.5) and dense (SG 6.7–7.0).

Tantalite-(Mn) on matrix.

COLUMBITE-(Fe)

An iron, manganese, niobium, tantalum, oxygen mineral, columbite-(Fe) resembles tantalite-(Mn) but is slightly less hard (H 6) and less dense (SG 5.2–6.8).

Columbite-(Fe) crystal.

TIN AND TUNGSTEN MINERALS

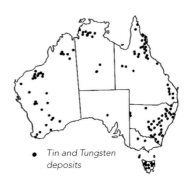

TIN AND TUNGSTEN tend to associate in mineral deposits. The main minerals are tin oxides and tungstates. They frequent pegmatites, veins and contact zones around granite bodies. Tin oxide often sheds into alluvial deposits. These minerals concentrate around New England, Albury–Ardlethan and Barrier Range, New South Wales; Atherton–Cooktown, Queensland; Bynoe–Pine Creek, Northern Territory; Pilbara, Norseman and Greenbushes, Western Australia; and in Tasmania.

• Tin and Tungsten deposits

TUNGSTATE minerals are largely iron-rich (ferberite), manganese-rich (hüebnerite) or calcium-rich (scheelite). Rare minerals include stolzite and raspite, named after Charles Rasp, discoverer of the Broken Hill ore body.

CASSITERITE

Called 'tin-stone', cassiterite is a tin and oxygen mineral. Often brown to black, it ranges into red, yellow, grey and white. Streak is white, greyish or brownish. Crystals (tetragonal) form squat pyramidal or prismatic shapes, commonly twins, or form needles and fibres. Grape-, kidney-, eye- and wood-like forms as well as rolled grains occur. Mostly opaque, with very bright lustre, it is hard (H 6–7) and dense (SG 6.8–7.1).

Cassiterite crystals.

STANNITE

A copper, iron, tin and sulfur mineral, stannite is steel-grey to iron black, with a blackish streak. Crystals (tetragonal) are typically twinned but stannite is mostly massive, granular or speckly in form. It is opaque, with a metallic lustre, somewhat soft (H 3.5) and moderately dense (SG 4.3–4.5).

Stannite in matrix.

91

FERBERITE

This iron, manganese, tungsten and oxygen mineral is dark grey to brownish black, with a near-black streak. Crystals (monoclinic) are often tabular, or wedge-shaped, with perfect cleavage and twinning. Opaque with a dull metallic lustre, the mineral is moderately hard (H 4–4.5) and dense (SG 7–7.5).

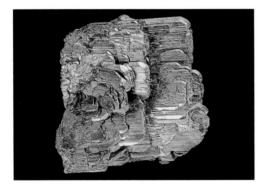

Ferberite crystals.

SCHEELITE

A calcium, tungsten and oxygen mineral, scheelite is white, grey, yellow, brown, or red, mostly pyramidal or tabular, with distinct cleavage and twinning. Kidney-like or granular forms occur. Transparent to translucent with glassy to very bright lustre, it is moderately hard (H 4.5–5) and dense (SG 5.9–6.1).

Scheelite crystal.

STOLZITE AND RASPITE

Stolzite is a lead, tungsten and oxygen mineral and grey, yellow, brown or red, with uncoloured streak. Crystals (tetragonal) are pyramidal, tabular or flattened. The mineral is opaque to translucent, resinous to quite bright in lustre, soft (H 2.5–3) and fairly dense (SG 8.3). The composition of raspite matches stolzite but crystals (monoclinic) are mostly tabular to elongate and show perfect cleavage and twinning. Colour is yellow-brown, yellow or grey, with very bright lustre. It is soft and dense like stolzite.

Above: Stolzite in matrix. Below: Reddish brown raspite with yellow stolzite.

IRON MINERALS: MAIN ORES

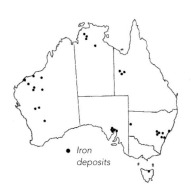

A ustralia has huge iron ore deposits in ancient banded
iron formations. These formed when Earth's atmosphere
oxygenated two billion years ago. The main ore minerals are
iron oxides and hydroxides, iron sulfides and iron carbonates.

Major iron ore deposits exist at Hamersley Range, Mount
Goldsworth–Shay Gap, Yampi Sound, Pompeys Pillar, Mount
Gould–Mount Hale, Weld Range, Mount Gibson, Koolanooka,
Koolyanobbing and Wundowie, Western Australia; Middleback
Ranges, South Australia; Constance Range, Queensland; and
Savage River, Tasmania. Smaller historic deposits lie in the
Sydney hinterland.

• Iron
deposits

IRON

Terrestrial iron is rare but extraterrestrial iron
occurs in iron and stony iron meteorites, which
impact from space. Formed 4.5 billion years ago
during planetary evolution, they have fallen ever
since. Rusty, pitted exteriors show metallic iron,
nickel alloy interiors when sliced (H 4–5 and
SG 7.3–7.8).

Grape-like hematite.

Iron meteorite.

HEMATITE

An iron and oxygen mineral, hematite is
dark grey to black, with a red streak. Crystals
(trigonal system) are often thick to thin tabular

shapes, with rhombic faces, and show lamellar
parting. Columnar, granular, grape-like and
stalactitic forms occur. Lustre is metallic to very
bright. It is hard (H 5.5–6) and moderately
dense (SG 4.9–5.3).

MAGNETITE

This iron and oxygen mineral is renowned for
its strong magnetism. Colour and streak are
black. Crystals (cubic) are typically octahedra

93

Minerals

Magnetite in its massive form.

or dodecahedra, or combinations, and can show twinning. Massive, lamellar and granular forms occur. The mineral is opaque, metallic to very bright in lustre, hard (H 5.5–6.5) and moderately dense (SG 5.1–5.2).

PYRITE

An iron and sulfur mineral, pyrite is pale brass-yellow, with a greenish black streak. Crystals (cubic) commonly show cubic or five-sided faces with striations, and are sometimes twinned. Lustre is metallic to bright and glistening. Massive, granular and sometimes radiating, kidney-like, globular and stalactitic forms develop. It is hard (H 6–6.5) and moderately dense (SG 4.9–5.1). A similarly composed mineral is marcasite, which has a different crystal system (orthorhombic).

Pyrite crystals.

PYRRHOTITE

Pyrrhotite is an iron and sulfur mineral. It is bronze-yellow to copper-red, with a grey-black streak, but the colour tarnishes. Crystals (hexagonal) are often tabular with cleavage. Massive to granular forms occur. Lustre is metallic, while hardness (H 3.5–4.5) and density (SG 4.6) are moderate. It can be weakly magnetic.

Pyrrhotite in its massive form.

ARSENOPYRITE

This iron and arsenic sulfur mineral is silver-white, tending to steel-grey, with a grey-black streak. Crystals (orthorhombic) are often prismatic, show cleavage and have a metallic lustre. Granular to compact forms occur. It is hard (H 5.5–6) and dense (SG 5.9–6.2).

Arsenopyrite on matrix.

IRON MINERALS: REDEPOSITED

Besides the main iron ore formations, Australia has redeposited iron ores. The latter include hydrous iron oxide minerals, generally called limonite. Deposited from groundwaters the minerals form irregular to pea-shaped lumps. These form laterites as soil deposits and gossans as alteration caps on ore bodies.

GOETHITE

An iron, oxygen and hydrogen mineral, goethite is yellow, red or blackish brown, with a brownish to yellow streak. Crystals (orthorhombic) are prisms, often flattened and

show a strong cleavage. Fibrous, lamellar, scaly, massive, kidney-like and stalactitic forms occur. Lustre is earthy to glistening. It is fairly hard (H 5–5.5) and moderately dense (SG 4.3).

Stalactitic goethite.

SIDERITE

This iron, carbon and oxygen mineral is grey, yellow, brown or red, with a whitish streak. Crystals (trigonal) form rhombs with curved faces, show perfect cleavage and twinning. They are generally translucent, with glassy to pearly lustre. Grape-like, globular, fibrous, compact or earthy forms occur. It is moderately hard (H 3.5–4) and moderately dense (SG 3.8–3.9).

Siderite crystals.

VIVIANITE

An iron, phosphorus, oxygen and hydrogen mineral, vivianite can be colourless, blue, green or near-black, with a colourless to bluish white streak. Crystals (monoclinic) form prisms with very good cleavage. It is transparent to translucent, very soft (H 1.5–2), and low in density (SG 2.6).

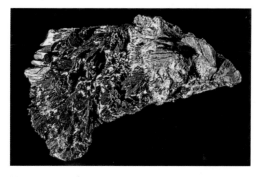

Vivianite crystals.

CHROMIUM MINERALS

Chromium minerals concentrate in rocks like peridotites and serpentinites. The main mineral is chromite and deposits appear in serpentinite belts in eastern Australia and in the Panton intrusion, Western Australia. Rare chromium alteration minerals form at serpentinite and metallic ore body contacts, as in western Tasmania.

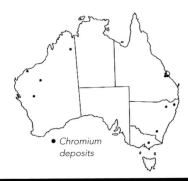

• Chromium
deposits

CHROMITE

A chromium, iron and oxygen mineral, chromite is brownish black to black, with brown streak. Crystals (cubic) are commonly octahedra, but massive, granular or compact forms occur. The mineral varies from opaque to translucent, with a metallic lustre, is hard (H 5.5) and moderately dense (SG 4.1–4.9).

Crocoite crystals, Dundas, Tas.

Chromite in matrix.

CROCOITE

This lead, chromium and oxygen mineral has attractive red colours and orange-yellow streak. Crystals (monoclinic) are usually prisms, sometimes needles, with distinct cleavage. They are translucent with a glassy lustre. Columnar to granular forms occur. It is soft (H 2.5–3) and dense (SG 5.9–6.1).

STICHTITE

This magnesium, chromium, carbon, oxygen and hydrogen mineral is lilac to rose-pink. The crystals (hexagonal) form scales or fibres. They are transparent with a pearly lustre, very soft (H 1.5–2) and low in density (SG 2.1–2.2).

Stichtite in massive form.

MANGANESE MINERALS

M anganese accompanies iron in many iron ore deposits in
Australia and is sometimes dominant. Manganese oxides
and hydrated oxides concentrate in alteration zones of lead, zinc,
copper ore bodies, as at Broken Hill and Overhang, Queensland.
A large deposit on Groote Eylandt in the Gulf of Carpentaria
contains small rounded bodies of manganese oxide deposited
from a previous sea. Pyrolusite is the main oxide mineral and
psilomelane the main hydrated oxide. Manganese carbonates,
phosphates and silicates also appear in ore bodies and in granitic
pegmatites.

• Manganese
deposits

PYROLUSITE
Pyrolusite is a manganese and oxygen
mineral. It is dark grey to bluish black with a
blackish streak. Columnar, granular, massive
and kidney-like forms occur but crystals
(orthorhombic) are rare. The mineral is opaque,
has a subdued metallic lustre, often soils the
fingers and is soft (H 2–2.5) and moderately
dense (SG 4.7–4.9).

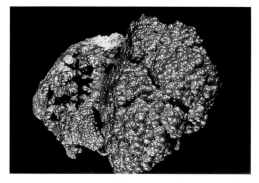

Grape-like psilomelane.

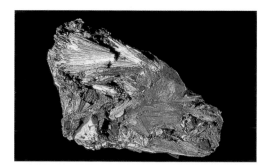

Pyrolusite crystal sheafs.

PSILOMELANE
This manganese, oxygen and hydrogen mineral
is dark grey to black, with a brownish streak.

Crystals are lacking and it shows a subdued
metallic lustre. It forms massive, grape-like or
stalactitic material. It is quite hard (H 5–7) and
moderately dense (SG 3.3–4.7).

ALABANDITE
A manganese and sulfur mineral, alabandite is
black with a green streak. Crystals (cubic) are
rarely distinct but show perfect cubic cleavage.
It generally has granular or massive form,
subdued metallic lustre and is moderately hard
(H 3.5–4) and moderately dense (SG 4.0–4.1).

Alabandite on matrix.

or needles, often radiating. They show good cleavage, are transparent to translucent and have a glassy lustre. The mineral is hard (H 6) and not very dense (SG 3.0–3.1).

RHODOCHROSITE

This manganese, carbon and oxygen mineral is rose-red, red, brown or yellow with a white streak. Crystals (trigonal) often form rounded rhombs, with perfect rhombic cleavages. They show some translucency and a glassy lustre. Globular, grape-like, columnar or crusty forms also occur. It is moderately hard (H 3.5–4.5) and moderately dense (SG 3.4–3.6).

Globular rhodochrosite.

INESITE

This is a calcium, manganese, silicon, oxygen and hydrogen mineral. Rose- to flesh-red and brown in colour, it has a white streak. Crystals (triclinic) are mostly elongated prisms

TRIPLITE

Inesite crystal sheafs.

This mineral contains manganese, calcium, magnesium, phosphorus, fluorine and oxygen. Brown to black-brown, it has a yellowish grey to brown streak. Crystals (monoclinic) are indistinct but have good cleavage. Generally opaque, this mineral can be massive and its lustre varies from resinous to very bright. It is moderately hard (H 4–4.5) and moderately dense (SG 3.4–3.8).

Triplite in its massive form.

NICKEL MINERALS

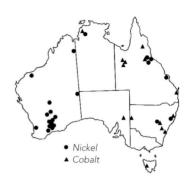

Western Australia possesses major nickel sulfide ores in its ancient 'greenstone' belts made of magnesium-rich submarine volcanic rocks and intrusions. The main deposits lie around Kambalda–St Ives, but similar deposits extend west towards Southern Cross and north to Wiluna. Alteration nickel deposits form in laterite at Greenvale, Queensland.

Pentlandite and, to a lesser extent, millerite dominate nickel-sulfides. Rare nickel-telluride minerals, like melonite, also occur. Alteration nickel minerals include carbonates, such as gaspéite.

● Nickel
▲ Cobalt

PENTLANDITE

This nickel, iron and sulfur mineral is bronze-yellow, with a bronze-brown streak. Crystals (cubic) are irregular with parting planes. Granular to massive forms predominate. The mineral is opaque, with metallic lustre, shows a curved fracture and is moderately hard (H 3.5-4) and moderately dense (SG 4.9–5.2).

Pentlandite in matrix.

MILLERITE

A nickel and sulfur mineral, millerite is brass to bronze-yellow, with a greenish black streak and grey iridescent tarnish. Crystals (trigonal) have good cleavage, form delicate radiating needles, hair-like growths, columnar tufts and part-globular forms. The mineral is opaque, with a metallic lustre, somewhat soft (H 3–3.5) and somewhat dense (SG 5.3–5.7).

Grape-like millerite.

MELONITE

This nickel and tellurium mineral is reddish white, with a dark grey streak and has a yellowish tarnish. Crystals (hexagonal) form plates and grains, and show cleavage. The mineral has a dull to glassy lustre. It is moderately hard (H 4.5–5) and moderately dense (SG 3.7).

Melonite in matrix.

GASPÉITE

A mineral containing nickel, carbon and oxygen, gaspéite is light green, with a yellow-green streak. Crystals (hexagonal) form small

Gaspeite in its massive form.

rhombs with rhombic cleavage. It has a dull to glassy lustre, is of moderate hardness (H 4.5–5) and has a moderate density (SG 3.7).

COBALT MINERALS

Cobalt minerals are sparse in Australia, apart from Mt Cobalt, Cloncurry, Queensland. They occur inland from Mackay to Cairns, and at Biggenden, Queensland; at Broken Hill, New South Wales; Read–Rosebery mines, Tasmania; and around Olary, South Australia.

ERYTHRITE

This colourful alteration mineral is a cobalt, arsenic, oxygen and hydrogen mineral. It is peach-blossom to carmine-red with a reddish white streak. Crystals (monoclinic) are often flattened prisms, with perfect cleavage. Fibrous, massive and crusty forms occur. The mineral is translucent with a silky lustre, it is soft (H 1.5–2.5) and not very dense (SG 3.3).

Spherical erythrite.

MAGNESIUM AND TITANIUM MINERALS

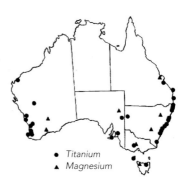

Titanium
Magnesium

MAGNESIUM minerals include rock-forming silicate mineral groups such as olivine, serpentine and talc. Carbonate, oxide and hydroxide minerals appear in serpentinites, sedimentary beds and metallic ores. Magnesite forms rich deposits at Kunnawarara, near Rockhampton in Queensland, and Thuddungra, near Young in New South Wales. Although lower in magnesium, dolomite deposits are sometimes worked. Talc at Mt Fitton in South Australia supplies material for industrial use and carving. Rare magnesium and ammonium-phosphate minerals come from guano found in bat caves.

TITANIUM minerals are dominated by the oxides rutile and ilmenite. They accompany many rocks but are mostly mined from coastal mineral sands. Other deposits occur at Olary and Flinders Range, South Australia and Cheyne, Western Australia.

MAGNESITE

This magnesium, carbon and oxygen mineral is white, pale yellow, grey or brown, with a white streak. Crystals (trigonal) are rare. Massive, granular, fibrous, nodular or earthy forms occur. It is opaque to transparent, with a glassy to silky lustre, slightly hard (H 3.4–3.5) and slightly dense (SG 3.0–3.1).

Magnesite nodule.

DOLOMITE

Calcium joins magnesium in this carbonate mineral, which is white, reddish or greenish, with a white streak. Crystals (trigonal) form rhombs with rhombic cleavage and build curved groups. Granular form is common. Transparent to translucent, it shows a glassy to pearly lustre, moderate hardness (3.5–4) and low density (SG 2.8–2.9).

Dolomite on marix.

TALC

A magnesium, silicon, oxygen and hydrogen mineral, talc is the softest mineral (H 1). White to greenish or brownish yellow, it shows a whitish streak. Crystals (triclinic) may form hexagonal plates or irregular leaves, but layered, fibrous, star-like, massive or compact forms dominate. It is translucent to transparent, with a pearly or waxy lustre, feels soapy and has low density (SG 2.6–2.8).

Talc in massive form.

NEWBERYITE

This is a rare magnesium, oxygen, hydrogen and phosphorus mineral. It forms glassy white transparent crystals (orthorhombic), shows good cleavage, is somewhat soft (H 3–3.5) and has low density (SG 2.1).

Newberyite crystals.

RUTILE

A titanium and oxygen mineral, rutile is brown-red, sometimes yellowish, bluish or black, with a pale brown streak. Crystals (tetragonal) form prisms to slender needles, show striations, distinct cleavage and knee-like twins. Opaque to transparent, with a metallic to very bright lustre, rutile is hard (H 6–6.5) and moderately dense (SG 4.1–4.3).

Rutile in matrix

ILMENITE

This titanium, iron and oxygen mineral is usually black with a brown–red streak. Crystals (trigonal) form thick tablets or thin plates. Massive, compact or granular forms occur. Opaque, with a curved fracture, it is hard (H 5–6) and fairly dense (SG 4.5–5).

Ilmenite crystal.

ALUMINIUM MINERALS

An abundant element, aluminium forms widespread minerals. Oxide minerals are prominent, for example, the spinel group and corundum, which includes gem varieties. Hydroxide and hydrated minerals form important aluminium ores, in bauxite deposits. Bauxite develops from intensive weathering of land surfaces that leaves aluminium-rich residues. Large deposits lie across the Gulf of Carpentaria and around Jarrahdale and Mt Saddleback, Western Australia. Aluminium silicates, such as andalusite, appear in metamorphic rocks, while hydrated aluminium silicates are common in clays.

• Aluminium deposits

SPINEL

This aluminium, magnesium and oxygen mineral grades into iron-bearing members. It ranges from red, blue, green, yellow-brown to black as iron content increases; it shows a white streak. Crystals (cubic) are typically octahedra, often twinned. Transparent to opaque, spinel is dull to glassy in lustre, shows a curved fracture and is quite hard (H 8) and moderately dense (SG 3.5–4.1).

Spinel crystal.

GAHNITE

An aluminium, zinc and oxygen mineral, gahnite is green, yellow, brown or black, with a grey streak. Crystals (cubic) are commonly octahedral and often twinned. Nearly opaque, with a greasy to glassy lustre, it is fairly hard (H 7.5–8) and moderately dense (SG 4.0–4.6).

Gahnite in matrix.

ANDALUSITE

Andalusite is an aluminium, silicon and oxygen mineral. It is white, grey, brown, red or green, with an uncoloured streak.

Crystals (orthorhombic) are commonly

squarish prisms with distinct cleavage. An altered of andalusite called chiastolite contains a distinctive cross of carbon in its structure. Radiating, massive and granular forms occur. It is transparent to opaque, glassy in lustre, hard (H 7.5) and not very dense (SG 3.1–3.2).

Altered andalusite.

BAUXITE

This is a mixture of aluminium, oxygen and hydrogen minerals, namely boemite, gibbsite and diaspore. It grades from white or grey into yellows and reds as iron impurities increase. Massive to rounded granular forms are common. Hardness is variable (2–4) and density is low (SG under 3).

Porous bauxite.

GIBBSITE

An aluminium, oxygen and hydrogen mineral, gibbsite is white, grey, green or red, with a whitish streak. Crystals (monoclinic) are typically tabular with strong cleavage. It shows spherical, stalactitic or crusty forms. Translucent, with a pearly lustre, it is soft (H 2.5–3.5) and low in density (SG 2.3–2.4).

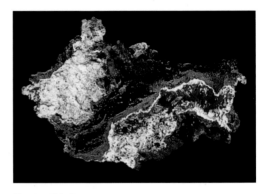

Crusty gibbsite.

DAWSONITE

This aluminium, sodium, carbon, oxygen and hydrogen mineral is colourless to white, with a white streak. Crystals (orthorhombic) form blades or needles, with perfect cleavage. Tufts, rosettes or crusts occur. It is transparent, with silky to glassy lustre, soft (H 3) and low in density (SG 2.4).

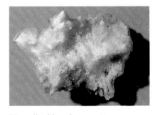

Needle-like dawsonite.

CALCIUM AND BARIUM MINERALS

CALCIUM minerals include carbonates, silicates, sulfates, phosphates and fluorides. Calcite forms limestones and cave decorations. Calcium silicates occur in igneous and metamorphic rocks, particularly 'cooked' limestone. Gypsum and calcite form in evaporite salt deposits and with fluorite in metallic ore bodies.

BARIUM is mostly found as the sulfate mineral baryte but it also occurs in carbonate, silicate and phosphate minerals. Significant deposits were mined around Adelaide, South Australia.

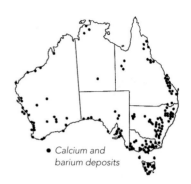

• Calcium and barium deposits

CALCITE

A calcium, carbon and oxygen mineral, calcite can be colourless (called 'Iceland spar'), white or many other colours, with a white to grey streak. Crystals (trigonal) vary widely; rhomb-, dogtooth- and nail-head shapes are common. Perfect rhombic cleavage and twinning is typical. Fibrous, lamellar, granular, compact, earthy, stalactitic, tube-like and nodular forms occur. Calcite is transparent to opaque, earthy to glassy in lustre, soft (H 3) and low in density (SG 2.7).

ARAGONITE

Aragonite's composition matches that of calcite. White or grey, sometimes yellow, green or violet, it has a white streak. Crystals (orthorhobmic) are often needle-like and twinned, with distinct cleavage. Globular, kidney-like, coral-like, columnar, stalactitic and crusty forms occur. Translucent to transparent, glassy, it is harder (H 3.5) and slightly denser (SG 2.9–3.0) than calcite.

Calcite crystals.

Aragonite crystal sheafs.

FLUORITE

This calcium and fluorine mineral has a spectrum of colours but it shows a white streak. The crystals (cubic) are usually cubes, but can be octahedra, dodecahedra or mixed forms. Fluorite has very easy, perfect octahedral cleavage. Massive granular and compact forms occur. It varies from translucent to transparent with a glassy lustre, and is moderately hard (H 4) and not very dense (SG 3.0–3.3).

Fluorite: cleaved crystals.

APATITE GROUP

These calcium, phosphorus and oxygen minerals are green to blue, sometimes white, and have a white streak. Crystals (hexagonal) are elongate to squat prisms or flattened. Globular, kidney-like fibrous, massive, granular

Apatite crystal in calcite matrix.

or compact forms occur. It is transparent to opaque with a glassy lustre, moderately hard (H 5) and slightly dense (SG 3.1–3.3).

GYPSUM

This calcium, sulfur, oxygen and hydrogen mineral is often white. Crystals (monoclinic) range from tabular to squat prisms, show pronounced cleavage and frequent twins. A compact form is alabaster. Transparent to opaque, with a pearly to glassy lustre, it is soft (H 1–1.5) with low density (SG 2.3–3.3).

Gypsum twinned crystal.

BARYTE

A barium, sulfur and oxygen mineral, baryte is usually white or grey, yellow, blue, red or brown, with a white streak. Crystals (orthorhombic) are tablets, or prisms, with perfect cleavage. Globular, fibrous, lamellar, granular, stalactitic and earthy forms occur. It is transparent to opaque, soft (H 2.5–3.5) and moderately dense (SG 4.3–4.6).

Barite crystal groups.

URANIUM MINERALS

A heavy radioactive element, uranium forms an array of minerals. Oxides and hydrous oxides represent the main ores, largely uraninite and its impure variety, pitchblende. Very large deposits occur around South Alligator River, Northern Territory, including some being mined (Ranger) or under controversial consideration (Jabiluka). Other primary deposits include Rum Jungle, Northern Territory; Mary Kathleen, Queensland; and Radium Hill and Olympic Dam, South Australia. In South and Western Australia, secondary deposits are located in former river channels. Uranium minerals include phosphates, arsenates, carbonates and silicates or involve titanium, vanadium, niobium and radioactive elements like thorium.

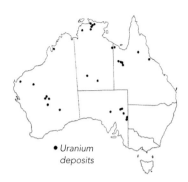

• Uranium deposits

URANINITE

This uranium and oxygen mineral is dark grey, brownish black or greenish black, with a grey, brown-black or green streak. Crystals (cubic) are typically octahedra, but the uncrystallised pitchblende variety shows massive, grape-like, kidney-like or banded form. Opaque, with subdued metallic lustre, uraninite is moderately hard (H 5–6) and dense (SG 7.5–9.7).

TORBENITE

A copper, uranium, phosphorus, oxygen and hydrogen mineral, torbenite shows an array of green colours, with a paler green streak. Crystals (tetragonal) form square tablets with perfect cleavage, but also exhibit sheet-like to scaly form. Torbenite is translucent to transparent with glassy to brighter lustres, is soft (H 2–2.5) and not very dense (SG 3.2).

Uraninite coated by saleiite.

Torbenite on matrix.

DAVIDITE-(La)

This mineral was named after the Australian geologist, T.W. Edgeworth David. In davidite, rare earth elements (lanthanum and cerium) join uranium, yttrium, titanium, iron and oxygen. It is dark brown to black, with dark grey brown streak. Crystals (hexagonal) are tablets or prisms but massive form is common. Opaque with a slight glassy lustre, it is hard (H 6) and moderately dense (SG 4.4–4.9).

Davidite in massive form.

CARNOTITE

A potassium, uranium, vanadium, oxygen and hydrogen mineral, carnotite is yellow to greenish yellow, with a yellowish streak.

Carnotite in matrix.

Crystals (monoclinic) are commonly platy with perfect cleavage. Compact, crusty and powdery forms occur. Carnotite shows a silky, pearly or dull lustre, is soft (H 2–2.5) and is moderately dense (SG 4.7).

SALEIITE

This magnesium, uranium, phosphorous, oxygen and hydrogen mineral is yellow, with a yellowish streak. Crystals (monoclinic) form thin rectangular tablets with perfect cleavage. Transparent to translucent, it is soft (H 2) and not very dense (SG 3.2–3.3).

Saleiite on matrix.

AUTUNITE

A calcium, uranium, phosphorus, oxygen and hydrogen mineral, autunite is yellow to green. Crystals (tetragonal) are thin, twinned tablets, scaly or crusty in form. It is transparent to translucent, soft (H 2–2.5) and not very dense (SG 3.1–3.2).

Autunite on matrix.

SILICATES: FELDSPARS

Silicates are the most abundant minerals. Feldspars, common silicate minerals, are particularly frequent in igneous and metamorphic rocks and less so in sedimentary rocks, which break down on weathering.

The basic feldspar structure gives different types of feldspar with many look-alike features. A frame of silicon and aluminium is held together by twice as much oxygen. Alkali and alkaline earth elements like potassium, sodium, calcium and barium fit into this framework. The alkali feldspars are rich in potassium and sodium, the plagioclase feldspars are rich in sodium and calcium.

SANIDINE

This potassium and sodium feldspar is colourless, white, grey, pale yellow or pink and like all feldspars shows a white streak. Crystals (monoclinic) are usually short prisms, often flattened with perfect cleavage and simple twinning. Massive to cleavable forms occur. Sanidine is translucent to transparent, has a glassy lustre and sometimes a bluish sheen (moonstone). It is hard (H 6) and not very dense (SG 2.6).

Sanidine in matrix.

ORTHOCLASE

Another potassium and sodium feldspar, orthoclase resembles sanidine. It differs only in its internal arrangements of atoms.

Orthoclase is often opaque and slightly harder (H 6–6.5) than sanidine but is similar in density (SG 2.6). It forms coarse crystals in rocks like granite whereas sanidine accompanies finer-grained volcanic rocks.

Orthoclase crystals.

MICROCLINE

A sodium and potassium feldspar, microcline is colourless, white, yellow pink, red or green with a white streak. Crystals (triclinic) form short prisms, with perfect cleavage. Finely banded multiple twinning crosses in two directions to give a 'tartan' effect. It can also interband with albite feldspar. It matches orthoclase in hardness and density (H 6–6.5; SG 2.6).

Microcline crystals.

'Anorthoclase' crystal.

LEAD-BEARING MICROCLINE

Rare microclines incorporate lead, giving a blue–green to green variety, sometimes called amazonite. This occurs at Broken Hill in New South Wales.

Lead-bearing microcline.

ALBITE–SANIDINE SERIES

Potassium-rich albite is known as 'anorthoclase' and can contain several percent of sodium and calcium. It can show a blue 'moonstone' sheen and appears in many volcanic rocks of eastern Australia. Transparent to translucent with a glassy lustre, it is moderately hard (H 6–6.5; SG 2.6).

PLAGIOCLASE SERIES

Plagioclase minerals extend from sodium-rich albite to calcium-rich anorthite and are mostly pale-coloured. Some sodium-rich varieties contain sparkling inclusions, while more calcium-rich varieties can show colour play. Crystals (triclinic) exhibit a characteristic finely banded multiple twinning. The minerals become slightly denser towards the anorthite end member. (SG 2.7–2.8).

Plagioclase crystals.

SILICATES: PYROXENES AND PYROXENOIDS

Pyroxene and related minerals frequent igneous and heat-altered metamorphic rocks. Their name comes from pyros ('fire') and xenos ('stranger') because the ancient Greeks thought such minerals were accidentally trapped in lavas.

They are made of silicon and aluminium bound with three amounts of oxygen. These chains link up with magnesium, calcium, iron, manganese, titanium and sodium. Pyroxenes include clino-pyroxenes (monoclinic or triclinic crystals) and ortho-pyroxenes (orthorhombic crystals).

AUGITE

This calcium, magnesium, aluminium, iron clino-pyroxene, sometimes includes titanium and sodium. It can be white, grey, green, brown or black, with a grey or brown streak. Crystals (monoclinic) form short, sometimes flattened, prisms. They exhibit typical pyroxene features, right angle cross cleavage and simple to multiple twinning. Opaque to translucent with a glassy lustre, augite is hard (H 5.5–6) and slightly dense (SG 3.2–3.6).

Augite in matrix.

ENSTATITE

A magnesium ortho-pyroxene containing minor iron, enstatite is colourless, grey, yellow, green, brown to black, with a grey to brown streak. Crystals (orthorhombic) form prisms, with good cleavage, but are often granular. It is opaque to transparent with a glassy lustre, hard (H 5–6) and slightly dense (SG 3.2–3.6).

Enstatite in matrix.

DIOPSIDE

Diopside crystals (green) in matrix.

This calcium, magnesium-rich clino-pyroxene is white to green, with a white to pale green streak. Crystals (monoclinic) are equant or prisms, sometimes tablets. It is opaque to transparent, glassy in lustre, hard (H 5–5.6) and slightly dense (SG 3.2–3.5).

HEDENBERGITE
A calcium, iron-rich clino-pyroxene, hedenbergite is pale to dark green or brown with a pale green to brown streak. Crystals (monoclinic) are equant, prisms or grains. It is opaque to translucent, glassy in lustre, hard (H 6) and moderately dense (SG 3.4–3.6).

Rhodonite crystals in matrix.

Hedenbergite crystals.

RHODONITE
This manganese, calcium, pryoxenoid silicate forms reddish, sometimes gemmy crystals (triclinic, H 5.5–6.5; SG 3.6–3.8)

WOLLASTONITE GROUP
These pyroxenoids include wollastonite, a calcium silicate, bustamite, a calcium, manganese, iron silicate and pectolite, a sodium, calcium silicate. Wollastonite mostly forms white, radiating monoclinic or triclinic crystals. Bustamite forms light pink to brown-red, tabular triclinic crystals, or hair-like forms. Pectolite forms white, pale brown, pink or blue triclinic crystals, often glassy to silky, radiating and spiky. Wollastonite and pectolite are moderately hard (H 4.5–5) and dense (SG 2.5–2.9), while bustamite is harder (H 5.5–6.5) and denser (SG 3.3–3.5).

Bustamite crystals.

SILICATES: AMPHIBOLES

Amphiboles abound in igneous and metamorphic rocks where geological environments provided water to assist amphibole formation. A Greek word, amphibolas ('ambiguous, doubtful') referred to the many amphibole minerals that are often difficult to tell apart.

In contrast to pyroxenes, the silicon and aluminium groups in amphiboles form double chains with oxygens. This leaves gaps where oxygen-hydrogen groups, the hydrous components, fit in. The chains are connected together by elements such as calcium, magnesium, iron, aluminium, titanium, sodium and potassium.

Like pyroxenes, amphiboles form as orthorhobmic, monoclinic or triclinic crystals, showing a good cross cleavage. However, these cleavages cross at 60° rather than at right angles. Amphiboles often form elongate or fibrous crystals.

'HORNBLENDE'

This old term now covers several calcium, magnesium, iron amphibole minerals which also contain sodium, potassium, titanium, hydroxyl and halide elements. They are white, green, brown or black, and have a pale streak. Crystals (monoclinic) are commonly twinned prisms. Columnar, fibrous, granular and massive forms occur. Opaque to translucent, they have a glassy to pearly lustre, are hard (H 5–6) and slightly dense (SG 2.9–3.4).

KAERSUTITE SERIES

More titanium-rich than 'hornblende' minerals, kaersutite is dark brown to black, with a brownish grey streak. Crystals (monoclinic) form short prisms, commonly twinned. Opaque to translucent, it is glassy in lustre, hard (H 5–6) and slightly dense (SG 3.2–3.3).

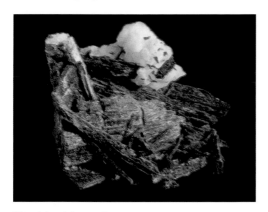

'Hornblende' crystals.

Kaersutite crystals in cavity.

TREMOLITE–FERRO-ACTINOLITE SERIES

The calcium, magnesium-rich member, tremolite, is colourless, white, grey or green, with a paler streak. Crystals (monoclinic) form prisms, blades or radiating groups. Compact, matted, fibrous and asbestos forms occur. Tremolite is translucent to transparent with a glassy to silky lustre, hard (H 5–6) and slightly dense (SG 2.9–3.2).

The iron rich members, actinolite and ferro-actinolite are green to black. Crystals (monoclinic) are commonly bladed, fibrous or splintery. It is transparent to translucent with a glassy to waxy lustre, hard (H 5–6.5) and slightly dense (SG 3.2–3.5).

Fibrous tremolite.

RIEBECKITE SERIES

A sodium, iron amphibole, riebeckite is light blue to blue-black with a bluish grey streak. Crystals (monoclinic) are lath-like, fibrous or form asbestos (crocidolite). It is opaque to translucent, glassy to silky in lustre, moderately hard (H 5–5.5) and slightly dense (SG 3.2–3.4).

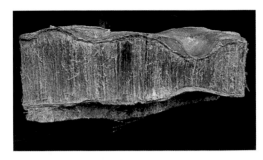

Riebeckite in asbestos form.

PYROSMALITE SERIES

Pyrosmalites are iron, manganese silicates with a ring-like structure, rather than chains. However, like amphiboles, the oxygen-hydrogen units fit within gaps. Yellow-grey, pink to red-brown, it shows a pale streak. Crystals (hexagonal) form stout prisms with perfect cleavage. It is translucent with a glassy to pearly lustre, moderately hard (H 4–5) and slightly dense (SG 3.1–3.2).

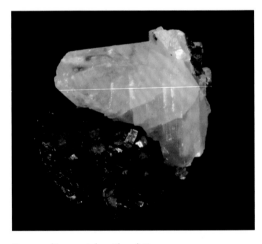

Pyrosmalite crystals with calcite.

SILICATES: ZEOLITES

Although variable in character, zeolites have two features in common. One is a frame of silicon and aluminium bound by twice the amount of oxygen. Attached to this are elements like sodium, potassium, calcium and barium. This frame forms lose cages. These cages give zeolite their second feature. Water and other molecules can pass in and out. When zeolites are heated, they lose their water and 'boil'. Zeolite means 'boiling stone'.

Zeolites feature in the widespread eastern Australian volcanic rocks, particularly basalts. Analcime, chabazite, phillipsite, natrolite and thomsonite are abundant. World-class colourful gmelinite, heulandite and stellerite come from Flinders in Victoria and Garawilla in New South Wales. Rare zeolites are found in Australia, mostly in microscopic crystals.

Microcrystalline clinoptilolite in altered volcanic ash beds at Werris Creek, New South Wales, is extracted for use as a pollutant-absorbing material. Zeolites also occur in Tasmanian dolerite and syenite intrusions, in volcanic sandstone along Bass Strait, in veins in Brisbane granite and in metamorphosed volcanics at Arkaroola in South Australia.

ANALCIME

A sodium zeolite, colourless to white, sometimes coloured, with a white streak. Crystals (cubic) are usually equant, but granular massive forms occur. It is transparent to near opaque, glassy in lustre, moderately hard (H 5–5.5) and low in density (SG 2.2–2.6).

Analcime crystals.

CHABAZITE GROUP

These calcium and sodium zeolites are white to flesh red, with an uncoloured streak. Crystals (trigonal) are often rhombs with distinct cleavage. They resemble cubes and also form inter-penetrating twins. More complex twins form lensoid shapes. It is transparent to translucent, glassy in lustre, moderately hard (H 4–5) and not very dense (SG 2.1–2.2).

Chabazite crystals.

115

GMELINITE

A sodium and calcium zeolite, gmelinite can be colourless, white, yellow, green, pink, red or brown, and it exhibits a white streak. Crystals (hexagonal) are mostly squat prisms or hexagonal plates, with good cleavage. Transparent to translucent, gmelinite has a glassy to dull lustre, moderate hardness (H 4.5) and is of low density (SG 2.0–2.2).

Gmelinite in matrix.

PHILLIPSITE GROUP

Phillipsites are potassium, sodium and calcium zeolites that sometimes also contain barium. They can be colourless, white, pink,

Phillipsite on matrix.

or yellow and exhibit a white streak. Crystals (monoclinic) are equant, blocky or elongate prisms and have a distinct cleavage. Complex twinning is typical and the crystals can form cross-like shapes. Radiating, spherical or coral-like forms can also occur. It varies from translucent to opaque and is glassy in lustre, moderately hard (H 4–4.5) and not very dense (SG 2.2).

STILBITE GROUP

These sodium and calcium zeolites are white, sometimes yellow, brown or red, with a white streak. Crystals (monoclinic) are thin tablets, with cross-like twinning, but they commonly occur in sheets. Radiating and globular forms can occur. Transparent to translucent with a glassy to pearly lustre, it is moderately hard (H 3.5–4) and low in density (SG 2.1–2.2).

Stilbite on matrix.

STELLERITE

This calcium zeolite is white, pink, orange, brown or red, with a white streak. Crystals (orthorhombic) are lamellar with perfect cleavage but also occur in spherical radiating aggregates. It is translucent, glassy in lustre, moderately hard (H 4.5) and low in density (SG 2.1–2.2).

show perfect cleavage and can take sheaf-like, globular or granular forms. Transparent to opaque with a glassy to pearly lustre, heulandite has slight hardness (H 3.5–4) and a low density (SG 2.2).

Stellerite crystals.

Laumontite on matrix.

LAUMONTITE

A calcium and sodium zeolite, laumontite is white, yellow, grey or red and shows an uncoloured streak. Crystals (monoclinic) are often prismatic with perfect cleavage and twinning. Columnar, diverging or radiating forms occur. Transparent to translucent with a glassy to pearly lustre, in air it decomposes to powder. Hardness is slight (H 3.5–4) and density low (SG 2.2–2.4).

HEULANDITE

Another calcium and sodium zeolite, heulandite is white, grey, brown or red, with a white streak. Crystals (monoclinic) are sometimes flattened,

Heulandite crystal sheafs.

117

NATROLITE

This sodium zeolite is colourless, white, grey or yellow, with a white streak. Crystals (orthorhombic) are elongate with perfect cleavage and commonly twin. Radiating needle-like, star-like and compact forms occur. It is transparent to near-opaque, glassy to pearly in

lustre, somewhat hard (H 5–5.5) and low in density (SG 2.2–2.3).

Natrolite in matrix.

MESOLITE

Mesolite is a sodium and calcium zeolite, related to natrolite and a calcium-rich zeolite, scolecite. It is colourless, white, yellow, pink, with a white streak. Crystals (orthorhombic) form needles, with perfect cleavage and twinning is common. Mesolite is transparent to translucent with a glassy to silky lustre,

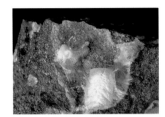

moderately hard (H 5) and low in density (SG 2.2–2.3).

Fibrous mesolite.

THOMSONITE GROUP

A calcium and sodium zeolite, thomsonite is colourless, white, pink, red or yellow, with a white streak. Crystals (orthorhombic) form blades or prisms, with twinning being common, but the forms are quite diverse. Transparent to translucent with a glassy to pearly lustre, it is somewhat hard (H 5–5.5) and not very dense (SG 2.2–2.5).

Thomsonite on matrix.

GONNARDITE

This sodium and calcium zeolite is coloured white, yellow or pink, with a white streak. Crystals (orthorhombic) are elongate prisms or needles. Gonnardite is transparent to near-opaque with a glassy, silky or dull lustre, is moderately hard (H 4.5–5) and not very dense (SG 2.2–2.4).

Gonnardite spheres on matrix.

SILICATES: MICAS

M icas and related minerals appear in many rocks where the presence of water aided their formation. The main mica characteristic is a pronounced cleavage that splits the mineral into sheets.

These sheets combine aluminium and silicon with two and a half times as much oxygen. They are linked with elements like potassium, sodium, magnesium, iron, aluminium, calcium and lithium.

Besides micas, other similar hydrous sheet-silicate groups include brittle micas, chlorites, vermiculites, serpentinites and talcs (see under magnesium minerals).

MUSCOVITE

A potassium mica, muscovite is colourless, grey, yellow, brown, green or violet, with an uncoloured streak. Crystals (monoclinic) are usually tabular and are commonly twinned. Book-like, star-like, feather-like, globular, scaly and compact forms occur. Transparent to translucent with a glassy, pearly or silky lustre, it is soft (H 2–2.5) and low in density (SG 2.7–3). It is called white mica.

Muscovite book-like form in matrix.

BIOTITE GROUP

These potassium, magnesium and iron micas are green brown to black, with an uncoloured streak. Crystals (monoclinic) are mostly tablets, short prisms, hexagonal sheets or scales. It is transparent to opaque, very bright, glassy or

pearly in lustre, soft (H 2.5–3) and not very

Biotite crystal.

dense (SG 2.7–3.1). It is called black mica.

LEPIDOLITE

A lithium and potassium mica, lepidolite is rose-red, violet or lilac, sometimes yellow, grey or white, with an uncoloured streak. Crystals (monoclinic) are either six-sided tablets or prisms, commonly twinned. Columnar or scaly forms occur. Transparent to translucent with a glassy to pearly lustre, it is moderately soft (H 2.5–4) and slightly dense (SG 2.8–3.3).

Columnar lepidolite.

CHLORITE GROUP

Chlorite group minerals are magnesium, iron and aluminium silicates with combined water. Typically dark green to green black, they have an uncoloured to greenish streak. Crystals (monoclinic) tend toward hexagonal shapes but massive, granular or scaly forms occur. They are transparent to opaque with a glassy to pearly lustre, soft (H 2–2.5) and low in density (SG 2.6–3.0).

Chlorite in matrix.

VERMICULITE GROUP

The vermiculite group minerals are magnesium, iron and aluminium silicates with combined water. They are grey, brown, gold or green to brown-black, and they have a white streak. Crystals (monoclinic) are rare and well-cleaved massive, scaly or worm-like forms are known to occur. They are transparent to opaque with an oily or earthy lustre, very soft (H 1–2) and rather low in density (SG 2.3–2.8).

Lamellar vermiculite.

CHRYSOTILE

This fibrous asbestos mineral belongs to the Kaolinite Serpentine Group and is a magnesium silicate containing water. The host rock is usually a green to black, poorly crystallised material, veined with greenish white to green fibres, with a silky lustre. It is soft to moderately hard (H 2.5–4) with a low density (SG 2.2).

Chrysotile asbestos veins.

OTHER SILICATES

Various other silicate minerals include gem varieties that are described under the gem minerals. Some are orthodox silicate structures, where silicon combines with four times the oxygen. They include garnets, olivines, zircon, titanite, topaz and kyanite. Staurolite is described below. Others are ring-like silicate structures, such as beryls, tourmalines and cordierite. Axinite is described below.

Among other silicates, some contain shared silicon, oxygen chains. Epidotes are prominent here. Other sheet-structure silicate minerals are abundant in well-developed crystals (apophyllite), represent rare species (bannisterite) or form poorly crystallised, common clay mineral groups (kaolinite) and swelling clay groups (nontronite).

EPIDOTE GROUP

As calcium, aluminium and iron hydrous silicates, epidotes are yellow-green or green to black, with an uncoloured to grey streak. Crystals (monoclinic) form bladed to needle-like prisms with perfect cleavage and twinning is common. Fibrous, granular and massive forms occur. It is transparent to opaque with a glassy, pearly or resinous lustre, hard (H 6–7) and slightly dense (SG 3.2–3.5).

Staurolite in matrix.

Epidote in matrix.

STAUROLITE

This iron and aluminium hydrous silicate is yellow-brown, red-brown and brownish black, with an uncoloured to greyish streak. Crystals (orthorhombic) are prisms, commonly flattened and often form cross-like twins. Translucent to opaque with a subdued glassy lustre, it is hard (H 7–7.5) and moderately dense (SG 3.6–3.8).

AXINITE GROUP

Axinite is a calcium, manganese, iron and boron silicate. The colour is purple-brown, grey or yellow, and it has an uncoloured streak. Crystals (triclinic) are usually broad and sharp-edged with distinct cleavage. It is transparent to translucent with a very glassy lustre, hard (H 6.5–7) and slightly dense (SG 3.3).

121

Axinite on matrix.

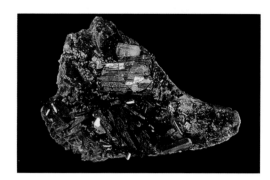

Bannisterite on matrix.

APOPHYLLITE GROUP

Apophyllites are potassium, calcium and fluorine hydrous silicates. They are white, grey, yellow, green or red, with a white streak. Crystals (tetragonal) range from squarish to tabular prism and pyramid combinations, with perfect cleavage. Transparent to near-opaque with a glassy to pearly lustre, it is moderately hard (H 4.5–5) and not very dense (SG 2.3–2.4).

Apophyllite crystals.

BANNISTERITE

Bannisterite is a rare potassium, calcium, manganese and iron hydrous silicate. Its colour is brown to black and it has a palish streak. Crystals (monoclinic) form prismatic blades and plates with perfect cleavage. It is translucent to opaque and exhibits a resinous lustre. It is of moderate hardness (H 4) and is low in density (SG 2.8).

KAOLINITE GROUP

A well-known clay mineral group, kaolinite is a hydrous aluminium silicate. It is white, grey or yellow, sometimes brown, blue or red, with a white chalky streak. Crystals (monoclinic) form scales or plates with perfect cleavage. Massive, compact, friable or slippery forms occur. Opaque with a pearly to earthy lustre, it is soft (H 2–2.5) and low in density (SG 2.6–2.7).

Kaolinite in its massive form.

CRYSTAL GALLERY

Azurite 'sun' in claystone, Areyonga, NT.

Cerussite, reticulated crystals, Broken Hill, NSW.

Copper crystals in matrix, polished face, Doolgunna, WA.

123

Crystal Gallery

Cassiterite crystal group, Pine Ridge, NSW.

Blue fluorite crystals on matrix, Renison Bell, Tas.

Pectolite, radiating crystals, Prospect, NSW.

GLOSSARY

accessory mineral A mineral present in a rock but not relevant to its classification.

alloy A mixture of incorporated metals.

alteration Change in the mineralisation of rock.

amphiboles Widespread, rock-forming silicate minerals with a double chain structure.

amphibolite A medium-grained, dark-coloured, metamorphic rock, rich in amphibole minerals.

angle of incidence The angle between a ray of light meeting a surface and the perpendicular to that surface.

annealing Heat treatment.

arsenates Minerals containing arsenic and oxygen units (1:4 ratio) that combine with metallic and other elements.

aventurescence A sparkling effect present in some minerals, produced by light reflecting off tiny mineral flakes under the surface.

basal Parallel to the base of a crystal.

basalt A common, dark-coloured, fine-grained, igneous volcanic rock.

bipyramid Two opposing pyramids joined by a common base.

birefringence Double refraction, caused by splitting of light rays entering a mineral.

brilliance The brightness of a cut gemstone, from light reflected off and through its facets.

bromides Minerals containing the element bromine combined with one or more metal elements and other elements.

carbonates Minerals containing carbon and oxygen units (1:3 ratio) that combine with metallic and other elements.

carbonatite An igneous rock, composed mainly of carbonate minerals and often rich in less common elements.

colour centre An irregularity in the crystal lattice that alters the selective absorption of light to produce a colour.

colour zoning Growth-related zones of colour in a mineral or gemstone.

concretion A rounded body, usually formed in a sedimentary deposit by the accumulation of mineral matter around a nucleus.

conglomerate Coarse-grained, sedimentary rock of rounded pebbles cemented together.

crystal A solid body with a regular atomic structure, which, under favourable conditions, develops regular planar faces.

crystal axes Imaginary lines of reference running through a crystal and intersecting in the centre at a fixed point. From these can be measured the mathematical relationship between the faces.

crystal faces The planes forming the developed boundaries of crystals.

crystal symmetry The symmetry of a crystal includes its centre, axes and planes of symmetry, which assign it to a crystal system.

crystal systems The seven main groups of crystal symmetry into which all minerals are classified.

crystalline Having the regular, internal properties of a crystal, with or without its outward form.

dendritic Branching, fern-like in form.

density A measurement of mass per unit of volume.

dichroism An ability, possessed by some doubly-refractive minerals, to show two different colours in different directions.

dolerite A medium-grained intrusive igneous rock of similar composition to basalt.

element A basic substance that cannot be simplified further by chemical means.

eluvial deposit An accumulation of residual ore minerals with little or no transport from the source rock.

end member The mineral at each end of a progressive mineral series.

equant Applied to a crystal with dimensions similar in all directions.

evaporites A group of sedimentary rocks laid down by the process of evaporation of water containing dissolved salts.

feldspars A family of widespread, rock-forming silicate minerals.

ferric iron Iron in the trivalent state, compared with ferrous iron in the divalent state.

fluorescence Visible light emitted by an object exposed to ultraviolet rays.

fluorides Compounds (minerals) containing the element fluorine combined with one or more metals and sometimes other elements.

geode An enclosed cavity in rock, lined with quartz or calcite crystals.

gneiss A coarse-grained, metamorphic rock, with alternate bands of light and dark-coloured minerals.

gossan A weathered rock, rich in iron oxide minerals, overlaying a sulfide deposit.

granite A coarse-grained, deep-seated, silica-rich, igneous rock.

greisen A coarse-grained, tin-bearing rock, similar to granite.

groundwater Water permeating rock masses, filling their pores and fissures.

habit The characteristic external shape of a mineral.

halides Minerals containing one or more halogen elements combined with metals and other elements.

halogens Non-metallic elements with similar general properties, including fluorine, chlorine, bromine, iodine and astatine.

heavy liquids Liquids heavier than water that are used for measuring the specific gravity of minerals and gemstones.

heavy minerals Minerals with a comparatively high specific gravity that causes them to settle in alluvial deposits.

hydrous Water-bearing.

hydroxides Minerals that contain hydroxyl (hydrogen-oxygen) units.

hydroxy Hydroxyl-bearing mineral that includes an oxygen atom combined with a hydrogen atom.

iodides Minerals containing the element iodine combined with metal and/or other elements.

igneous One of the three main rock types; formed by the cooling and solidifying of magma or lava.

inclusion Foreign matter—solid, liquid or gas—enclosed in a mineral or gemstone.

intrusion A body of igneous rock invading pre-existing rock below the surface.

ironstone A sedimentary rock rich in iron oxide minerals.

kimberlite A low-silica, igneous rock from the mantle, that can be diamond bearing.

labradorescence A type of iridescence seen in plagioclase feldspar, caused by reflection of light from sub-surface layers.

lamellar Composed of thin layers, plates, scales or lamellae.

lamproite An igneous rock, rich in potassium and magnesium, that can contain mantle material and, sometimes, diamond.

Late-stage Forming at a late stage in the crystallisation sequence of magma.

laterite A rock, formed by the leaching of previous rocks, rich in iron and aluminium oxide minerals.

lensoid Thick at the middle and thinning out at each edge.

magma Hot, molten material below the Earth's surface that, on cooling, forms igneous rocks.

mantle The zone of the Earth below the crust and above the core.

matrix The 'parent rock' in which minerals have crystallised or been transported.

metalliferous Metal bearing.

metamict A term describing a mineral whose crystalline structure has broken down, due to internal bombardment by radiation.

metamorphic One of the three main rock types; formed by the alteration of pre-existing rock.

metamorphism The alteration of pre-existing rock, sometimes by contact with intrusive molten magma or lava.

meteorite Planetary material from the asteroid belt or beyond that travelled through Earth's atmosphere and fell to its surface.

micas Widespread rock-forming silicate minerals that have a sheet-like structure.

microcrystalline Made up of sub-microscopic crystals.

micromounts Small, mounted mineral specimens, best seen under a microscope.

mineral An inorganic substance with an ordered, atomic lattice and a chemical formula that is fixed within narrow limits.

mineral series Minerals with similar structure but progressive differences in chemistry between two end members.

noble metals An alchemist's term for metals most resistant to chemical reaction—gold, silver, mercury and the platinum group.

nodule A small, rounded body, weathered out of softer material.

octahedron An eight-sided crystal, each side being an equilateral triangle.

ore body A continuous mass containing economic quantities of ore.

ornamentals Opaque minerals or rocks, prized for their surface colours and patterns and used for ornamental objects.

oxides A group of mineral compounds containing oxygen combined with one or more metallic elements.

parti-coloured Gemstones cut from crystals whose colours have altered during growth.

parting The tendency of crystals to separate along certain planes of weakness, other than true cleavage planes.

pegmatite A type of granite with rare elements, sometimes forming large gem crystals.

peridotite A coarse-grained, igneous rock composed largely of olivine.

phosphates Minerals containing phosphorus and oxygen units (2:5 ratio) that combine with metallic and other elements.

pleochroism The ability, possessed by doubly-refractive minerals, to show two or three different colours in different directions.

primary ore One that has remained practically

Glossary

unchanged since its original formation.

prism Columnar form made up of crystal faces around a vertical axis.

pseudomorph A mineral that has replaced and taken the outward form of another mineral.

pyramid A form of triangular sloping faces that meet at the vertices of a crystal, forming a pyramid-like end(s) to the crystal.

pyroxenes Widespread rock-forming silicate minerals that have a single chain structure.

quartzite A metamorphic rock consisting mainly of quartz.

rhomb(us) An oblique, equilateral parallelogram.

rhyolite Fine-grained, siliceous volcanic rock.

schist A metamorphic rock, made of flaky minerals, which splits readily.

secondary ore The alteration or secondary concentration products of primary ore, often formed through weathering processes.

sedimentary One of the main rock types, formed by deposition of sand, grit and clay fragments eroded from pre-existing rocks.

serpentinite A metamorphic rock composed largely of serpentine minerals formed by hydrous alteration of olivine-rich rocks.

silicates A group of minerals containing silicon and oxygen units that combine with metallic and other elements.

skarn A metamorphic rock derived from limestone or dolomite infiltrated by contact with magmatic fluids.

specific gravity The weight of a substance compared with the weight of an equal volume of pure water.

striations Parallel lines or grooves on a crystal or rock surface.

sulfates Minerals containing sulfur and oxygen units (1:4 ratio) combined with metallic and other elements.

sulfides Minerals containing sulfur and one or more metallic elements.

syenite A deep-seated, coarse-grained igneous rock with less silica than granite.

tektite Glassy, fused rock produced by meteoritic impact that flung melt into space before re-entry to Earth's surface.

tetrahedron A crystal form that has four faces, each being an equilateral triangle, and which belongs in the cubic system.

termination The crystal form at the end of a prism.

trace elements Elements occurring in lesser but detectable quantities in minerals and rocks.

Troy ounce A unit of weight, equal to 31.103 grams, used for precious metals.

tungstates Minerals containing tungsten and oxygen units (1:4 ratio) that combine with metallic or other elements.

twinning Crystal growth occurring in two directions, symmetrically, from a single plane.

type specimen The specimen from which the original description of a species was taken, serving as a permanent reference point. **vitreous** Similar surface reflectivity to glass.

weathering The process of gradual breakdown undergone by rocks and minerals as a result of physical and chemical processes.

zeolites Widespread silicate minerals that have cage-like structures containing loose water.

Buyer's Guide To Gemstones

Gemmologists are often asked the question, 'What should I look for when buying a gemstone?' There are particular features to look for in individual gemstones, but there is an important piece of advice to remember when buying any gemstone. Always buy from an established and reputable point of sale, where you can get information about the stone you are considering buying. If you buy, ask for a receipt stating the identity of the stone, how much it weighs and its price. This will not present a problem to any reputable gem dealer or jeweller and gives a customer security if any problem should arise later. Gemstones have a more or less established price, according to their inherent quality, at any one point in time. A relentless search for a bargain may lead buyers to less scrupulous dealers and, ultimately, inferior or fraudulent goods.

What to look for in a gemstone

In coloured stones, look for an intense and attractive colour, neither too light nor too dark; in colourless stones look for purity and clarity. Inclusions are a natural feature of minerals and gemstones and help to establish a gemstone's natural origin. However, they should be visible only through a jeweller's hand lens (with 10x magnification) and not to the naked eye. If inclusions are large enough to be eye-visible, they can interfere with the passage of light through the stone, reducing its brightness. An exception is made for emeralds, however, since they are almost always included—sometimes quite heavily. Emeralds are valued for the intensity and beauty of their colour rather than for their clarity, which is usually less than in other gemstones. Brightness is important in a gem, so make sure your stone is lively. Ask to see a number of examples and make comparisons with colour and brightness in mind.

Synthetic and imitation stones abound and can be extremely difficult to distinguish from natural materials. Even a gemmologist may need to use a microscope or a more high-tech method to establish whether a stone is natural or synthetic. Besides synthetic stones, buyers should be aware of the widespread treatment of gemstones, today. Artificial staining of porous materials such as agate and turquoise is prevalent. Heat treatment is used routinely to improve the colour of sapphire, ruby or aquamarine (it is permanent and often undetectable). A number of stones, including topaz and diamond, are often exposed to artificial radiation to improve or change their colour. Surface-reaching fractures in diamond, ruby or emerald are sometimes filled with another material, to improve clarity and make the stone more marketable. Other more sophisticated methods of improving gemstones are continually being devised.

Buying from a reliable source repays gem lovers with the confidence that they have chosen well and avoided the pitfalls of synthetic and fraudulently treated stones.

ADDITIONAL SOURCES

Atlas of the Mineral Occurrences and Petroleum Fields of the Northern Territory, Northern Territory Geological Survey, Darwin, 1999.

Birch, W.D. (Ed.), *Minerals of Broken Hill*, Broken Hill City Council, 1999.

Birch, W.D. and Henry, D.A., *Gem Minerals of Victoria*, Mineralogical Society of Victoria, Melbourne, 1997.

Bonewitz, R.L., *Rock and Gem*, Dorling Kindersley, London, 2008.

Bottrill, R. and Baker, W.E., *A Catalogue of the Minerals of Tasmania*, Bulletin Geological Survey Tasmania 73.

Busbey, A.B., Coenraads, R.R., Roots, D. and Willis, P.M., *Rocks & Fossils*, Rev. ed., Readers Digest Press, Surry Hills, Sydney, 2011

Coupe, R., *Australia's Gold Rushes*, New Holland, Sydney, 2000.

Chaline, E., *Fifty Minerals that Changed the course of History*, Allen & Unwin, Sydney, 2010.

Cram, L., *Beautiful Opals: Australia's National Gem*, Cram, Lightning Ridge, 1999.

Fetherstone, J.M., Stocklmayer, S.M. & Stocklmayer, V.C., *Gemstones of Western Australia*, Mineral Resources Bulletin 25, 2013.

Francis, G.L., *Minerals of Iron Monarch*, One Steel, Whyalla, 2010.

Hall, C., *Gemstones*, Dorling Kindersley, London, 2000.

Landman, N.H., Mikkelsen, P.M., Bieler, R., Bronson, B., *Pearls, A Natural History*, Harry N. Abrams, New York, 2001.

Opal, The Phenomenal Gemstone. Clifford, J. et al. (Ed.), Lithographie, LLC, Connecticut, 2007.

Pabian, R., Jackson, B., Tandy, P. & Cromartie, J., Agates, *Treasures of the Earth*, Natural History Museum, London, 2006.

Post, J. E., *The National Gem Collection*, Smithsonian Institution & Harry N. Abrams, New York, 1997.

Queensland's Metalliferous and Industrial Minerals 2010, Queensland Government, Brisbane, 2010.

Schumann, W., *Minerals of the World*, Sterling, New York, 1999.

Schumann, W., *Gemstones of the World* (4th ed.), Sterling, New York, 2011.

Sofianides, A.S. & Harlow, G.E., *Gems & Crystals from the American Museum of Natural History*, Simon & Schuster, New York, 1990.

Sutherland, L., *Gemstones of the Southern Continents*, Reed Books, Sydney, 1991.

Tait, K., *Gems & Minerals*, Earth Treasures from the Royal Ontario Museum, Firefly Books, Toronto, 2011.

Voillot, P., *Diamonds and Precious Stones*, Thames & Hudson, London, 1998.

Ward, F., *Opals*, 3rd ed., Gem Book Publishers, Bethseda, MD, USA, 2011.

Online sources:
www.mindat.org
www.gemdat.org

SPECIMEN DETAILS

GEMSTONES

Diamonds

Yellow diamond crystal (11.47 ct); Ellendale, WA.

Argyle diamond concentrate (largest ~ 0.35ct); Smoke Creek, Argyle, WA.

Argyle colour range; Argyle Mine, WA.

Stones from Argyle Pink Diamond Tender, 2013; (largest 2.02 ct)

Copeton diamond crystals (largest 1ct); Copeton, NSW.

Faceted Copeton diamonds (largest 1ct); Copeton, NSW.

Australia's largest diamond crystal (104.73 ct); Merlin Mine, NT.

Sapphire

Sapphire crystal (2 × 1 cm) in basalt; Anakie, Qld.

Sapphire crystals (largest 28 ct); eastern Australia.

Colour-zoned sapphire crystal (3 cm across); Inverell, NSW.

Faceted sapphire (3.56 ct); Inverell, NSW.

Carved sapphire (47 ct); eastern Australia.

Zircon inclusion (~ 3mm) in sapphire; Lava Plains, Qld.

Fancy-coloured Sapphire

Sapphire colour range (each 5 mm); Inverell, NSW.

'Kingsley sapphire' (162 ct); Fancy Stone Gully, Rubyvale, Qld.

Faceted golden sapphire (7.20 ct); Tomahawk Creek, Qld.

Faceted orange sapphire (3.50 ct); Kings Plains, Inverell, NSW.

Star sapphire (1cm across); Anakie, Qld.

Faceted colour-change sapphire (34 ct); Anakie, Qld.

Ruby

Ruby crystal (2 cm across) in gneiss; Harts Range, NT.

Harts Range ruby cabochons (each 5 mm); Harts Range, NT.

Faceting quality ruby crystals (2–6 mm); Barrington Tops, NSW.

Faceted ruby (0.80 ct); Barrington Tops, NSW.

Ruby– sapphire suite crystals (2-6 mm); Barrington Tops, NSW.

Rubies set in ring; Barrington Tops, NSW.

Precious Opal

Opal seam (35 × 12 cm); Andamooka, SA.

Black opal (10 ct); Lightning Ridge, NSW.

Black opal (12 × 10 mm) in ring; Australia.

Light opal; Australia.

Opal cameo (6 × 3.5 cm); Coober Pedy, SA.

Crystal opal (3 x 2 cm); Andamooka, SA.

Boulder Opal

Boulder opal on matrix (8 x 6 cm); Qld.

'Yowah nut' opal (7 × 6 cm); Yowah, Qld.

Boulder opals showing red flash; same opals showing blue; Quilpie, Qld.

'Galaxy Opal' (10 × 10 cm); Jundah, Qld.

Specimen Details

Other Opal

Volcanic opal (oval cabochons to 1 cm); Tintenbar, NSW.

Hyalite opal (whole specimen 15 × 15 cm); Dalby, Qld.

Green common opal (15 x 10 cm); Bulong, WA.

Common opal replacement of wood (6 x 4 cm); Lightning Ridge, NSW.

Opalised gastropod shell (2.5 cm across); White Cliffs, NSW.

Opal 'pineapple' (8 cm across); White Cliffs, NSW.

Crystallised Quartz

Quartz crystals (whole specimen 30 × 20 cm); Howell, NSW.

Rock crystal: two generations (36 cm long); Magill, SA.

Faceted rock crystal (188 ct); Oban, NSW.

Smoky quartz crystals (25 × 25 cm); Kingsgate, NSW.

Faceted smoky quartz (50 ct); Oban, NSW.

Rutilated quartz cabochons (length 3 cm); Tingha, NSW.

Coloured Quartz

Amethyst crystal group (14 cm across);

Amethyst sceptres (to 7cm long); Tarana, NSW.

Faceted amethyst (1.56 ct); Wyloo Station, WA.

Amethyst crystals (9 x 9 cm); Kuridala, Cloncurry district, Qld.

Faceted citrine (102 ct); Oban, NSW.

Citrine and cairngorm (largest stone 102 ct); NSW.

Quartz crystals and faceted stones; Australia.

Fine-grained Quartz

Chalcedony (Polished oval 5 cm long); Australia.

Agate nodules (largest 7 × 6 cm); Agate Creek, Qld.

'Whale' agate; Penstock, Tas.

Chrysoprase (14 × 6 cm); Marlborough, Qld.

Banded Jasper; Tuena, NSW.

Silicified casuarina trunk; Bushy Park, Derwent Valley, Tas.

Composite Quartz

Thunder egg (12 × 10 cm); Agate Creek, Qld.

Quartz geode (14 cm across); Agate Creek Qld.

Jaspilite; Marble Bar, WA.

Tiger's eye (12 cm across); Hammersley, WA.

Tiger iron; Wittenoom, WA.

Siliciophite; Pilbara, WA.

Emerald and Other Beryl

Emerald crystal in schist (crystal 3 x 2 cm); Menzies, WA.

Faceted emerald (0.90 ct); Torrington, NSW.

Emerald-zoned crystal (largest 5 × 1 cm) and cut stone (7.18 ct); Torrington, NSW.

Green beryl (136 ct); Torrington, NSW.

Aquamarine crystal (8.5 × 3.5 cm) and cut stone (11.72 ct); Mt Surprise, Qld.

Golden beryl crystal (4 cm long); Heffernans Mine, Torrington, NSW.

Topaz

Topaz crystal (3 cm long) on matrix; Killiekrankie, Flinders Island, Tas.

Blue-zoned topaz crystal (4 x 4 x 4.5 cm); Oban, NSW.

Faceted blue topaz (184 ct); Oban, NSW.

Blue topaz cleavage (9 cm across) with cut stone (184 ct); Oban, NSW.

Faceted colourless topaz (68 ct); Oban, NSW.

Faceted colourless topaz (larger stone, 22.80 ct); Ebor, NSW.

Garnet

Colour-zoned andradite crystals in matrix; Yetholme, NSW.

Almandine crystal (3 x 2.5 cm); Mount Swan area, NT.

Spessartine on matrix (8.5 × 6 cm); Broken Hill, NSW.

Grossular crystal (2cm across); Harts Range, NT.

Grossular colour range (4 mm); Harts Range, NT.

Faceted hessonites (each 3.50 ct); Harts Range, NT.

Zircon

Zircon crystal on matrix (7 × 5.5 cm); Mud Tank, Strangways Range, NT.

Mud Tank zircons (6 mm); Mud Tank, Strangways Range, NT.

Faceted zircons (round stone 7.64 ct); Mud Tank, Strangways Range, NT.

New England zircons (to 7 mm); Kings Plains, New England, NSW.

Low-uranium zircons (2-6 mm); NSW.

Higher uranium zircons (2-6 mm); NSW.

Silicate Gemstones, pp. 61-64

Olivine crystals in volcanic bomb (11 × 8 cm); Mt Leura, Vic.

Faceted peridot (9 ct); Cheviot Hills, Qld.

Yellow andesine crystal (4 × 2.5 cm); Springsure, Qld.

Faceted andesine feldspar (33.34 ct); Hogarth Range, NSW.

'Sunstone' feldspar; Harts Range, NT.

Faceted blue tourmaline (14.65 ct); Kangaroo Island, SA.

Nephrite jade; Tamworth, NSW.

Nephrite jade carving (5 × 7 cm); Cowell, SA.

Nephrite jade pendant; Tamworth, NSW.

Faceted rhodonite (2.24 ct); Broken Hill, NSW.

Polished rhodonite slice (15 × 10 cm); Danglemah, NSW.

Chrysocolla veins; Australia.

Silicate Gemstones, pp. 65-66

Prehnite (10 cm across); Prospect, NSW.

Faceted prehnite (3 × 2.5 cm); Wave Hill, NT.

Cordierite crystal (7.5 x 2.5 cm); Valley Bore, NT.

Faceted iolite (8 ct); Valley Bore, NT.

Kyanite crystals (to 9 cm); Harts Range, NT.

Faceted sphene (8.45 ct); Strangways Range, NT.

Other Gemstones

Turquoise seam (6 cm high); Ammaroo Park, NT.

Polished malachite (10 × 6 cm); Burra, SA.

Variscite (15 × 8 cm); Meekatharra, WA.

Apatite, rough (3 × 2 cm) and faceted (2.15 ct); Strangways Range, NT.

Faceted green fluorite (147 ct); Rumbsby's Mine, The Gulf, Emmaville, NSW.

Faceted pink fluorite (437 ct); Bundarra, NSW.

Polished cassiterite (82 ct); Elsmore, NSW.

Specimen Details

Pearls

Most Australian cultured pearls are from the north-western coast of WA.

ORNAMENTAL GALLERY, pp. 71–72

Agate nodule halves (larger 7.5 x 6.5 cm); Boggabri area, NSW.

Agate: polished slice (12 x 8 cm); Agate Creek, Qld.

Agate: polished half (12 x 6 cm); White Rock, Drake, NSW.

Agate: polished slice (10 x 5.5 cm); Katherine, N.T.

Blue lace agate (7.5 x 4.5 cm); Monto, Qld.

'Ribbonstone' chert; (155 x 85 cm); Mooka Station, Carnavon Shire, WA.

MINERALS

Gold & Platinum Minerals

Crystallised gold on quartz (9 x 4 x 3.5 cm); Kalgoorlie, WA.

Octahedral gold crystals (2 × 2 cm); Home Rule, NSW.

Gold nugget (20 × 7 cm); Ovens River, Vic.

Calaverite (7 × 4 cm); Kalgoorlie, WA.

Krennerite (15 × 5 cm); Great Boulder Mine, Kalgoorlie, WA.

Platinum nugget (1.5 × 1 cm); Fifield, NSW.

Silver Minerals

Silver in matrix (FOV 1 × 2 cm); Proprietary Mine, Broken Hill, NSW.

Dyscrasite on matrix (5 × 5 cm); Consols Mine, Broken Hill, NSW.

Stephanite (10 × 4 cm); Consols Mine, Broken Hill, NSW.

Proustite on matrix (21 × 14 cm); Junction Mine, Broken Hill, NSW.

Chlorargyrite, bromian (FOV 2 × 4 cm); Proprietary Mine, Broken Hill, NSW.

Iodargyrite (4.5 × 4 cm); Proprietary Mine, Broken Hill, NSW.

Copper Minerals: Common Alterations

Copper with gypsum (12 × 4 × 3 cm); Mt Elliot, Qld.

Copper crystals (FOV 3 × 2 cm); Proprietary Mine, Broken Hill, NSW.

Azurite (8.5 × 3 cm); Broken Hill, NSW.

Malachite on matrix (10 × 8 cm); Nymagee, NSW.

Malachite and azurite (5.5 × 3 cm); Proprietary Mine, Broken Hill, NSW.

Chrysocolla on matrix (30 × 25 cm); Dorothy Mine, Mungana, Qld.

Copper Minerals: Main Ores

Cuprite (largest crystal, 1cm); Proprietary Mine, Broken Hill, NSW.

Bornite (3 × 4 cm); North Mt Lyell, Tas.

Chalcopyrite (9 × 6.5 cm); Wallaroo Mines, Kadina, SA.

Covellite in matrix (4 × 4 cm); Moonta Mine, SA.

Chalcocite (4 x 2.5 cm); Telfer Mine, WA.

Tetrahedrite (3 × 2 cm); Little Plant Mine, Emmaville, NSW.

Copper Minerals: Rarities

Atacamite in matrix (9.5 × 5cm); Moonta, SA.

Linarite on matrix (7 × 4 cm); British Mine, Broken Hill, NSW.

Marshite (9.5 × 7.5 cm); Broken Hill, NSW.

Clinoclase (FOV 2.8 × 2 cm); Dome Rock

Mine, Olary Province, SA.

Conichalcite on matrix (12 × 6 cm); Dome Rock Mine, Olary Province, SA.

Pseudomalachite (8 × 4.5 cm); West Bogan Copper Mine, Tottenham, NSW.

Lead Minerals: Main Ores

Primary galena ore (10.5 × 10 cm); Broken Hill, NSW.

Secondary galena (11 × 7 cm); South Mine, Broken Hill, NSW.

Cerussite twin (7 × 2.8 cm); Broken Hill, NSW.

Anglesite (7 × 4 cm); Broken Hill, NSW.

'Chrome' cerussite (FOV 2 × 2 cm); Comet Mine, Tas.

Dundasite (11.5 × 5.5 cm); Dundas, Tas.

Lead Minerals: Common Alterations

Pyromorphite (6 × 4.5 cm); Kangiara Mine near Yass, NSW.

Mimetite on matrix (15 × 5 cm); Mt Bonnie Mine, NT.

Phosgenite on matrix (2.5 × 5 × 3 cm); Dundas, Tas.

Molybdenum Minerals

Molybdenite (5.5 × 5 cm); Wolfram Camp, Mt Arthur, Qld.

Wulfenite on matrix (6 × 4 cm); Whim Well Mine, Whim Creek, Pilbara, WA.

Zinc & Cadmium Minerals

Sphalerite (6 × 5 cm); Broken Hill, NSW.

Chalcophanite in matrix (7 × 5.5 cm); Broken Hill, NSW.

Smithsonite (7 × 6.5 cm); Broken Hill, NSW.

Tarbuttite (5.5 × 5 cm); Reaphook Hill, Flinders Range, SA.

Scholzite in matrix (40 × 20 cm); Reaphook Hill, Flinders Range, SA.

Greenockite on matrix (4 × 3 cm); Woodlawn Mine, Near Tarago, NSW.

Antimony, Bismuth & Tantalum Minerals

Stibnite (7 × 4 cm); Freehold Mine, Hillgrove, NSW.

Kermesite (6 × 4.5 cm); River Tree, Drake, NSW.

Bismuth (8.5 × 5 × 3 cm); Wolfram Camp, Mt Arthur, Qld.

Bismuthinite (7 × 5 cm); Allies Mine, Deepwater, NSW.

Tantalite-(Mn) on matrix (7 × 6 cm); Spargoville, WA.

Columbite-(Fe) crystal (8 × 4 cm); Spargoville, WA.

Tin & Tungsten Minerals

Cassiterite on matrix (7 × 5 × 5 cm); Elsmore, NSW.

Stannite in matrix (7 × 5.5 cm); Conrad Mine, Howell, NSW.

Ferberite (6 × 6 cm); Wolfram Camp, Mt Arthur, Qld.

Scheelite (5 × 5 cm); Nundle, NSW.

Stolzite in matrix (10 × 9 cm); Proprietary Mine, Broken Hill, NSW.

Raspite (largest crystal, 1.3 cm); Proprietary Mine, Broken Hill, NSW.

Iron Minerals: Main Ores

Iron meteorite (100 × 50 cm); Yenberrie, NT.

Hematite (7 × 5 cm); near Alice Springs, NT.

Magnetite (5 × 5 cm); Fine Flower Mine,

Specimen Details

Lyonsville, NSW.

Pyrite (10 × 6 cm); Mt Stewart Mine, Leadville, NSW.

Pyrrhotite (6 × 4 cm); Nairne Pyrite Mine, Bruckunga, SA.

Arsenopyrite (10 × 8 cm); Webbs Consols Mine, Strathbogie, NSW.

Iron Minerals: Redeposited

Goethite (10 × 12 cm); Beltana, SA.

Siderite (9 × 6 cm); Consols Mine, Broken Hill, NSW.

Vivianite (8 × 5 cm); Wannon Falls, Vic.

Chromium Minerals

Chromite (FOV 4.5 × 4.2 cm); near Barraba, NSW.

Crocoite (10 × 5 cm); Adelaide Mine, Dundas, Tas.

Stichtite (12 × 10 cm); Dundas, Tas.

Manganese Minerals

Pyrolusite (8 × 4 cm); Woodie Woodie, WA.

Psilomelane (6.5 × 5 cm); near Walcha, NSW.

Alabandite on matrix (12 × 7 cm); Zinc Corporation Mine, Broken Hill, NSW.

Rhodochrosite (largest hemispheres, 1 cm across); North Mine, Broken Hill, NSW.

Inesite (5 × 5 cm); Zinc Corporation Mine, Broken Hill, NSW.

Triplite (30 × 8 cm); Macmahon Quarry, Olary Province, SA.

Nickel Minerals

Pentlandite (14 × 10 cm); Mariner's Mine, Widgiemooltha, WA.

Millerite (15 × 10 cm); Agnew Nickel Mine, Agnew, WA.

Melonite in matrix (7 × 5 cm); Kambalda, WA.

Gaspéite (10 × 8 cm); Otter Shoot, Kambalda, WA.

Cobalt Minerals

Erythrite (7.5 × 6 cm); Mt Cobalt, Selwyn, Qld.

Magnesium & Titanium Minerals

Magnesite (20 × 10 cm); Mt Palmer, Bingera, NSW.

Dolomite on matrix (7 × 6 cm); Hillgrove, NSW.

Talc (10 × 6 cm); Mt Fitton, Flinders Range, SA.

Newberyite (FOV 6 × 4 cm); Skipton Caves, Vic.

Rutile in matrix (12 × 5 cm); Blumberg, Flinders Range, SA.

Ilmenite (3 × 2 cm); Arkaroola Bore, Flinders Range, SA.

Aluminium Minerals

Spinel (3 × 2 cm); near Mt Davies, SA.

Gahnite in matrix (5 × 6 cm); Consols Mine, Broken Hill, NSW.

Andalusite (5 × 4 cm); Mt Howden, Olary Province, SA.

Bauxite (20 × 10 cm); Gove, NT.

Gibbsite (12 × 7 cm); Adelaide Mine, Dundas, Tas.

Dawsonite (9 × 6 cm); Muswellbrook, Hunter Valley, NSW.

Calcium & Barium Minerals

Calcite crystals (18 x 16 x 10 cm); Cliefden, Carcoar, NSW.

Aragonite (7.5 × 5 cm); old basalt quarry, Footscray, Vic.

Fluorite (FOV 20 × 17 cm); Rumsby's Mine, Emmaville, NSW.

Apatite crystal (4.5 cm) in matrix; Broken Hill, NSW.

Gypsum (9 × 7.5 cm); South Mine, Broken Hill, NSW.

Baryte (15 × 8 cm); Broken Hill, NSW.

Uranium Minerals

Uraninite (10 × 8 cm); Rum Jungle, NT.

Torbenite (FOV 2.5 cm); El Sherana Mine, NT.

Davidite (10 × 5 cm); Radium Hill, Olary Province, SA.

Carnotite in matrix (10 × 5 cm); Yeelirrie, WA.

Saleiite on matrix (14 × 7.5 cm); Ranger Number 1 Mine, NT.

Autunite on matrix (12 × 6 cm); Mt Painter, SA.

Silicates: Feldspars

Sanidine in matrix (10 × 10 cm); Peak Range, Clermont, Qld.

Orthoclase (15 × 6 cm); Bolivia, New England, NSW.

Microcline (20 × 10 cm); Bolivia, New England, NSW.

Microcline, lead-bearing (10 × 8 cm); South Mine, Broken Hill, NSW.

'Anorthoclase' crystal (7 x 4 x 2.5); Mount Franklin, Vic.

Plagioclase crystals (largest 5 cm); Hogarth Range, NSW.

Silicates: Pyroxenes & Pyroxenoids

Augite in matrix (10 × 8 cm); Little Island, Lord Howe Island, NSW.

Enstatite in matrix (10 × 9 cm); Barraba, NSW.

Diopside in matrix (8 × 5 cm); Yinnietharra Station, Gascoyne Region, WA.

Hedenbergite (8 × 5 cm); North Mine, Broken Hill, NSW.

Rhodonite (largest crystal 1.5 cm); Broken Hill, NSW.

Bustamite in matrix (10 × 9 cm); NBHC Mine, Broken Hill, NSW.

Silicates: Amphiboles

'Hornblende' (8 × 6 cm); Mary Kathleen, Qld.

Kaersutite (FOV 1.5mm); Bullenmerri, Vic.

Tremolite (9 × 6.5 cm); Mt Fitton, Flinders Range, SA.

Riebeckite (15 × 5 cm); Wittenoom, WA.

Pyrosmalite in matrix (5 × 4 cm); Zinc Corporation Mine, Broken Hill, NSW.

Silicates: Zeolites, pp. 115-17

Analcime on matrix (7 × 3 cm); Emu Quarry, Prospect, NSW.

Chabazite (9 × 9.5 cm); Emmaville, NSW.

Gmelinite in matrix (9 × 7 cm); Flinders, Vic.

Phillipsite on matrix (11 × 6 cm); Richmond, Vic.

Stilbite on matrix (5 × 4 cm); Zinc Corporation Mine, Broken Hill, NSW.

Stellerite (8 × 3 cm); Mt Mitchell Station, Tambar Springs, NSW

Zeolites, pp. 117-18

Laumontite on matrix (8.5 × 5 cm); Broken Hill, NSW.

Heulandite (11 × 6.5 cm); Garawilla, NSW.

Natrolite in matrix (6 × 5 cm); Ardglen, NSW.

Specimen Details

Thomsonite on matrix (10 × 5 cm); road-side quarry, Cassilis, NSW.

Mesolite in matrix (5.5 × 5 cm); Cassilis, NSW.

Gonnardite on matrix (20 × 10 cm); Collingwood, Vic.

Silicates: Micas

Muscovite, book-like form, in matrix (11.5 × 6 cm); Harts Range, NT.

Biotite (7 × 4 cm); Harts Range, NT.

Lepidolite (3 × 5 cm); Grossmont, near Coolgardie, WA.

Chlorite in matrix (8 × 8 cm); Anderson's Creek, Beaconsfield, Tas.

Vermiculite (10 × 12 cm); Bulong, WA.

Chrysotile in matrix (20 × 15 cm); Lucknow, NSW.

Other Silicates

Epidote in matrix (30 × 20 cm); Harts Range, NT.

Staurolite in matrix (40 × 12 cm); Thackaringa, Broken Hill, NSW.

Axinite on matrix (7.5 × 5 cm); Colebrook Hill, Rosebery, Tas.

Apophyllite (10 × 6 cm); Broken Hill, NSW.

Bannisterite (12 × 5.5 cm); Zinc Corporation Mine, Broken Hill, NSW.

Kaolinite (10.5 × 9.5 cm); Coorabin clay mines, Oaklands, NSW.

CRYSTAL GALLERY, pp. 123–124

Azurite ' sun' in claystone (disc 11 cm across); Mabunka Mine, Areyonga, NT.

Cerussite, reticulated crystals (17 x 14 x 10 cm); Broken Hill, NSW.

Copper crystals in matrix: polished slice (10.5 x 9 cm); DeGrusser Mine, Doolgunna, WA.

Cassiterite crystals (9 x 6 x 5 cm); Pine Ridge, Copeton, NSW.

Fluorite crystals on pyrrhotite, with calcite overgrowth (12 x 6 x 6 cm); Renison Bell, Tas.

Pectolite: radiating crystal groups (12 x 12cm); Prospect, NSW.

*FOV = Field of View

PHOTOGRAPHIC CREDITS

T = top, b = bottom, c = centre, l = left, r = right.

Jim Frazier: pp , 6, 11, 13, 24b, 28t, 30b, 33bl, 33br, 34tr, 36tl, 36cr, 37br, 39bl, 39br, 40bl, 41bl, 41br, 42tl, 42tc, 42bl, 43tl, 43bl, 45tr, 45cr, 46cl, 47cl, 48bl, 49br, 50tl, 50tr, 50br, 51bl, 51tr, 51br, 54cl, 54tr,56tr, 57tr, 58tl, 58tr, 58cr, 59bl, 59tr, 59br, 60tl, 61bl, 62tl, 62tr, 63tl, 63tr, 64tr, 64br, 65cl, 66tr, 67bl, 68cl, 68br, 106tl Carl Bento: pp 29, 49tr, 52cl, 52tr, 52bl, 56cr, 57br, 76tr, 77tr, 81cl, 81tr, 82cl, 82br, 83br, 84cl, 84br, 86bl, 87br, 88tl, 88bl, 89bl, 89br, 90tl, 90bl, 90tr, 91bl, 92tl, 92bl, 95tr, 97cl, 98tl, 100br, 102bl, 104cr, 105br, 108cr, 111bl, 111br, 112bl, 112br, 114bl, 115bl, 115br, 116cl, 116bl, 116br, 117tl, 119bl Stuart Humphrey: pp 2, 5, 7, 34cl, 35br, 39tr, 40cr, 41tr, 43cr, 44cl, 44tr, 46bl, 46tr, 47tr, 47br, 48cl, 50bl, 53tl, 53tr, 53br, 55bl, 55tr, 55br, 61br, 62bl, 62br, 64bl, 65tr, 65br, 68tr, 68cr, 71-2, 73bl, 110br, 118tl, 123-4 Australian Museum Collection: pp 44br, 73br, 74tl, 74bl, 74br, 79cr, 82bl, 85tr, 86cr, 87bl, 88tr, 90br, 93cr, 94tl, 94bl, 95cl, 96br, 98tr, 98br, 99br, 101bl, 101br, 102tr, 102br, 103br, 104tl, 104br, 106br, 108tc, 108br, 109bl, 114tr, 117cr, 118tr, 120br, 121bl, 121tr John Fields: pp26, 27bl, 27br, 35bl, 74tl, 75tl, 75br, 76tl, 76br, 77bl, 79bl, 81br, 92cr, 92br, 96tr, 98bl, 100tl, 109tr, 110cl, 112tr, 114br, 120tr Paul Ovendon: pp 30t, 32b, 80cl, 80br, 88br, 91br, 94cr, 94br, 95br, 96cl, 97bl, 99bl, 102tl, 103bl, 112tl, 113bl, 118bl, 118tr Gregory Millen: pp 67cr, 68tl, 77tr, 100bl, 105bl, 108bl, 118br, 120tl Rick Bolzan: pp 33t, 78tl, 78br, 80tl, 83bl, 84tr, 106cr, 117br, 122bl, 122tr Cate Lowe: pp 93bl, 104bl Heather McLennan: pp 63br, 78cl, Rudy Weber: pp 31b, 32t, 36bl, 38cr, 40tl, 48bl, 56cl, 66cl, 66br Gayle Sutherland: pp 10, 34bl, 38tl, 38bl, 38tr, 60bl, 60cr George Smith: pp 57bl, 78br, 80tr, 83tl, 106bl Rio Tinto Diamonds: pp front cover, 12, 24t, 31cl, 31tr Lin Sutherland: pp 25t, 28b Ross Pogson: pp 6br, 107br State Library, Victoria: pp 25b Sally Robinson: p 26t Paspaley Pearling Co: pp 69-70 Julian Hollis: p 113br Bill Birch: p 110tr Murray Thompson: p 45bl Anthony Smallwood: p 27tl

139

INDEX

Index